THE 7~DAY
CHAKRA
WORKOUT
Handbook

The 7-Day Chakra Workout Handbook
Anita Revel

ISBN 978-0-557-35006-3

Published by Now Age Publishing Pty Ltd :: NowAgePublishing.com
PO Box 1800, Margaret River, Western Australia 6285

Some tips before commencing:

1. If you get into one particular life aspect and find that you need to
    spend more time there, please do take the time out that you need to
    address any issues that arise. The author honours you for the
    courage in taking this journey, so please remember to honour
    yourself too, and above all, be gentle.

2. If you can't do the seven days consecutively, don't worry. Just
    remember, everything happens at the perfect time for the perfect
    reason.

3. By commencing with this program, it is implied that you
    understand that the information in this book is for educational
    purposes only. It should not be considered as a substitute for
    consultation with a licensed healthcare professional or as a
    replacement for any medical treatment.

THE 7~DAY CHAKRA WORKOUT Handbook

ANITA REVEL

Books by the same author

Moon Goddess, Manifest Your Dreams
(Goddess.com.au   August 2006)

Selena's Crystal Balls,
A Magical Journey Through the Chakras
(Goddess.com.au   March 2007)

Outing the Goddess Within,
One Girl's Journey With 52 Guides
(Goddess.com.au   January 2008)

The 7-Day Chakra Workout
(ChakraGoddess.com   April 2008)

Sacred Vigilance, Wide-Awake Meditation
(Goddess.com.au   September 2008)

Goddess At Play, A Journal For Self-Discovery & Play
(Goddess.com.au   February 2009)

What Would Goddess Do?
A Journal for Channelling Divine Guidance
(Goddess.com.au   March 2009)

BOTIBOTO: Beautiful On The Inside, Beautiful On The Outside, An
Empowerment Story for Well-Rounded Women
(Now Age Publishing eBook April 2009)

The Goddess DIET, See a Goddess in the Mirror in 21 Days
(Now Age Publishing June 2009)

The Goddess Guide to Chakra Vitality, 3rd edition
(Now Age Publishing August 2009)

Goddess Makeover, A Home-Study Course in Personal Values,
Self-Actualisation and Divine Revellion
(Now Age Publishing February 2010)

Table of Contents

Ancient Theories, Modern Practice

I was first introduced to the world of chakras in my late twenties via a series of workshops run by a sacred singer and teacher. Life began to make sense once I incorporated the various theories into my daily practices – I became more settled, I was happier on my path and I awakened to the hundreds of blissings being gifted to me every day.

Over time, I was guided to adapt the basic principles of the chakra system to work with the seven essential aspects of life – security, abundance, power, love, truth, trust and joy. This new method became my code for living. It was a mix of the old (the ancient, sacred chakra teachings) and the new (my interpretation and application into modem life.) For the first time I found it possible to marry the Spiritual with the Corporate and remain true to both walks of life. In doing so, the 7-Day Chakra Workout eventually evolved.

I think one of the advantages of this Workout is that you don't need to drop everything in order to do it. You can simply incorporate the suggested activities into your regular life as it is now, so that you can form new, healthy habits and an inspired life for yourself.

I hope you enjoy *The 7-Day Chakra Workout* as much as I enjoyed creating it.

Love and blissings,

Anita Revel

Before You Begin

The next seven days of your life is not meant to be an all-consuming marathon of meditation and yoga. Quite the opposite, I have designed this program with the intention of offering you many choices to design a program to suit you best. Aim to work with the seven essential tools each day where you can, and whatever other tools you can use as well.

Each person's journey through the chakras is unique and personal, so honour your intuition about what tools are right for you. During my own journey, I found these following tools to be very helpful, and therefore recommend them to you now.

1.   A journal where you can record your thoughts of heart-felt honesty, and your journey through the seven chakras.

Jot down your reactions, reflections, explorations and experiences as you progress through the Workout. It is my intention that your journal will become a beautiful record where you can form your own empowered beliefs based on your own findings and revelations.

2.   A table, window ledge or room that is all yours, where you can build an altar or sacred space.

Clean the area before you start with salt water and pure intentions. Over the seven days it is my hope that you create an emotional connection with your space. Make it *your* sacred space where honesty and affirmative energy flow.

3.   An open heart and a faith system.

In this Workout I refer to the Universe as the ultimate provider of all that is good and holy, but you may choose to replace 'Universe' with your own faith system to suit you. No matter whether it be God/dess, the angels, Buddha, Allah, your higher self or even the fairies at the bottom of the garden, have faith that you deserve what you ask for.

Ways You Can Do This Workout

Individually

Choose a week where you don't have major distractions – it is already enough that you will be spending a lot of time focussing on your needs and true nature without having to worry about things like your mother-in-law visiting, a child starting school or the stresses of selling your home.

Remember to be gentle with yourself during the Workout. Aim for balance with your regular life and the activities suggested during the week. Ideally, you will find that your daily life becomes enhanced and enriched by the activities – *not* overwhelmed by them.

If you find yourself making excuses or compromises, or unable to find the time or resources, ask yourself why this is – what aspect of your true self are you avoiding in sabotaging your success? Be honest and forgiving in the unveiling of concealed truths.

I suggest that if you stop the Workout at any time during the seven days, revisit your promise to self and your commitment to your success. Also consider spending as long as is needed healing the chakra where the blockage occurred.

If you have managed to keep the energies of the previous chakras active during this healing time, continue on with the Workout. If, however, you begin to feel restless or anxious about your process, slow down and begin the Workout again at a pace to suit yourself.

If you find yourself emotionally distressed at any time, please do not hesitate to seek the assistance of a healer.

One day a week over seven weeks

A one-day-a-week series of workshops with a group* can be very enlightening and a great fun way to approach the Workout. I do recommend that all background reading is completed by participants prior to commencing the series of workshops. That way you can get started on the Workout from the first workshop on a level playing field.

I also recommend that participants read each day's work prior to attending the workshop. This will help them prepare emotionally and practically for the work ahead.

If you can manage, an ideal way of setting this up, would be to start the series on a Sunday and conduct each workshop on the designated day – that is, work on the sacral chakra on the Monday of the following week, the solar plexus on the Tuesday in the week thereafter, and so on.

As a retreat*

Allow nine days to complete the Workout, including the arrival day and download/departure day. On the day of arrival, have everyone read the background notes in this book, set up their space for their altar, and meet together at sunset for an opening ceremony (great fun).

For a weekend retreat, spend no more than an hour discussing each of the chakras and doing activities to balance them.

Group work is motivating, insightful and enables bonding, but also allow personal-space time each day for participants.

On the day of departure, allow the morning for processing Day Seven's evening activities, debriefing the group, tying up loose ends, and cleaning up.

A friendly reminder: this work is copyright and cannot be copied for distribution. Please contact Now Age Publishing for permission to run a retreat program based on any part of this guide.

Preparing Yourself for the Workout

Before reading the balancing approaches in this book, promise your Self one thing. *That in seeking to accomplish a positive life, you will align your attitude with the vision of what it is you seek to attract.*

This means letting go of old habits of self-criticism, mockery, and negative treatments. It means choosing self-acceptance and love, and dusting off your wings as you prepare to fly.

Believe that you have unlimited potential for abundance, love, security and joy. Maintain this mindset as you journey through this Workout for your highest good.

Now, this isn't just lip service I'm suggesting. I'm absolutely serious when I ask you to promise me to do your utmost to align your attitude with your desired outcome. As Oprah Winfrey said, "When your purpose and personality are in true alignment, that is power. I believe the only power that really matters is authentic power[1]..."

Making a Promise to Your Self

> # In seeking to accomplish a positive life, I hereby align my attitude with the vision of that which I seek to attract.

If this promise doesn't resonate, use the worksheet provided over the page so you can explore your intentions. Write down what it is you aim to achieve out of this Workout. From this space, you can play with your wording to formulate an easy-to-remember promise that aligns your heart-space wholeheartedly to achieve your bliss.

---

1   Bazaar magazine, August 2001

Worksheet – My Promise

How I want my life to look once I've completed the Workout:

What I need to release in order to align myself with this goal:

☐ fear of judgement   ☐ self-loathing ☐ self-criticism
☐ state of denial ☐ subservience ☐ shame
☐ guilt   ☐ lack of self-worth

☐ Others

What I am inviting into my life to align myself with this goal:

☐ trust in self   ☐ connection with intuition
☐ self-acceptance ☐ total honesty ☐ empowerment
☐ pride   ☐ joy   ☐ self-esteem

☐ More

My promise to myself:

Whether you're happy with my suggested promise or you're intending to create your own, make it personal and meaningful. Hand-write it, paint it or use glue-and-glitter to declare it. However you do it, just *mean* it!

Quiz: Am I Out of Balance?

Being absolutely, positively, totally and ruthlessly honest with yourself, give yourself a rating for each of the following statements. Get it? No white lies, denial or shame!

Complete all seven sections before peeking at the Answers. A '5' rating indicates that you resonate wholeheartedly with the statement, whereas a '1' rating says you disagree or are foreign to this concept. Your total scores will give you an idea of where you need to focus on to bring your chakras back into balance.

Section 1

Statement	My rating				
My home is my haven; people are welcome as long as they respect my space and my rules	5	(4)	3	2	1
I mostly have fond memories of school, particularly of my teachers	5	(4)	(3)	2	1
My present family and circle of friends mean everything to me	(5)	4	3	2	1
I recognise 'fear' as a sign-post for my next juicy challenge	5	4	(3)	(2)	1
I describe myself as a grounded person; I'm in touch with nature and common sense	5	(4)	(3)	2	1
The sound of drumming sets my feet tapping uncontrollably	(5)	4	3	2	(1)
I find comfort knowing that when 'shit happens', it is simply fertiliser for the next stage in my life	5	(4)	(3)	2	1

Add your ratings to get a total score: 23   28

Section 2

My appetite is good and not just for food –   5 4 (3) 2 1
sex and fun are also priorities

I have regular and easy bowel habits   5 (4) 3 (2) 1

When I look in the mirror I like what I see   5 (4 (3) 2 1

I have a nickname for my breasts, such as   5 4 3 2 (1)
'the girls'

Belly-dancers are sexy   (5) 4 3 2 1

As an adult, I have rolled Jaffas down the   5 4 3 2 (1)
aisle of a movie theatre

I dislike the term 'control freak'; I actively 5 (4 (3) 2 1
avoid being labelled as one

Add your ratings to get a total score: 19   23

Section 3

I act on my intuition always   5 (4 (3) 2 1

I used to be ashamed of a certain thing, but   (5) 4 3 (2) 1
now I'm not

I am responsible for my actions and am able   (5 (4) 3 2 1
to accept the consequences

I recognise that butterflies in my belly are   5 4 (3) 2 1
firing me up for success

I have plenty of energy   5 (4 (3) 2 1

I can describe myself in three words   (5) 4 3 2 1

People don't like me? Ha! Their problem   5 (4 (3) 2 1

Add your ratings to get a total score: 24   28

Section 4

I have fully grieved the loss of loved ones who have passed away   5 (4) 3 2 1

Referring to someone's spouse as their 'better/other half' is demeaning   5 4 3 2 (1)

I am guilt-free about my choices   5 4 (3) 2 1

I tend to trust first, ask later   (5) 4 (3) 2 1

People come and go from my life, and I do not fear when they go   5 (4) 3 2 1

I accept compliments easily – I deserve them, in fact!   5 4 (3) 2 1

Self-acceptance brings me joy   (5) (4) 3 2 1

Add your ratings to get a total score: 25   22

Section 5

People respect my personal space   5 (4) 3 (2) 1

I love singing in the shower   5 4 (3) 2 1

These words are taboo in my vocab: can't, couldn't, should   5 (4) (3) 2 1

I know how to say 'eff-off' without hurting anyone's feelings   5 4 3 (2) (1)

I am able to ask for a pay-rise when I know I am deserving   5 4 (3) (2) 1

Gossip bores me   5 (4) 3 (2) 1

I seldom interrupt others when they are speaking   5 4 (3) (2) 1

Add your ratings to get a total score: 16   22

Section 6

Statement	My rating				
I describe myself as an optimist	5	④	3	2	1
Fantasies are fun and healthy	⑤	④	3	2	1
Toxic thinking is for suckers	⑤	④	3	2	1
Paying attention to detail is easy	5	④	3	②	1
I understand that what I think, do or say is exactly what I attract	5	④	3	2	1
I've always been a quick-learner	5	④	③	2	1
There is always room for silence in my life – I am comfortable with it	5	④	3	②	1

Add your ratings to get a total score: 24 29

Section 7

Statement	My rating				
When my head hits the pillow, I go to sleep easily; I remember dreams	⑤	4	③	2	1
I star-gaze regularly	5	4	③	2	1
Coincidences and synchronicity happens to me a lot	5	④	3	2	1
Whatever happens, happens at the perfect time and for the best	5	4	③	2	1
I communicate daily with my higher self, god/dess, angels, the Universe	⑤	4	3	2	①
Headaches? What are they?	5	④	3	②	1
I volunteer for community projects on a regular basis	5	4	3	②	①

Add your ratings to get a total score: 20 23

Quiz Answers

Section 1: Base Chakra

30-35   Oh hail, Earth Mother! I honour you for your constant and calm nature and the stabilising influence you bring to those around you. You are very grounded.

15-29   Freddy Mercury once sang, "We will, we will, rock you!" You too will rock everyone's world once you settle down and find more stability in your life. I use the word 'rock' purposefully here – who or what is your rock, and why? Add these qualities to your life.

7-14   I'm surprised you stuck around long enough to finish the quiz. You're probably so busy trying to work out where to go next in your life, you're as flighty as all get-out. It's time to energise your base chakra!

Section 2: Sacral Chakra

30-32   Good for you! Play, laugh, abundance and 'curves' are great mottos. You are good friends with your body and probably reclaim words considered modern vulgarities – fanny, pussy, vaj, twat, etc. Keep relishing intimate sex and your feminine divine.

15-29   Consider ways you can loosen up a little, release those remnants of self-loathing and embrace the plethora of joys life has to offer. If you've been wearing a poker face for too long, smile!

7-14   Admit it. You've been called a control freak more than once in your life. Never fear, once you realise there is no shame in laughing and playing, loving your body, being rich, and throwing your hands up in mock defeat occasionally, you'll be fine.

Section 3: Solar Plexus Chakra

30-35   'Spontaneous' may well be your middle name, but as you
         know yourself so well, you are quite prepared to accept
         the consequences of your actions. You are proud to own
         your actions because they define you.

15-29   It's only natural to feel anxious about some situations, but
         at the end of the play, it's really all about you. Why are
         you so concerned about what other people think of you
         anyway? Know who you are to attract people of equal
         integrity.

7-14   Have you got a PUPPET sign on your forehead? Without
         any personal boundaries or understanding of who you
         really are, it's no wonder you are being used, abused and/
         or taken for granted.

Section 4: Heart Chakra

30-35   Oh come here and give me a hug! I just know you're as
         open to receiving my love as I am to receiving the love
         you have to give. Oh what beautiful and sacred balance
         you offer us all with your Three G-forces of Love:
         Gratitude, Grace and Generosity.

15-29   Knock knock! This is your little love-faery here to remind
         you that love is the Universe's greatest power. You may as
         well give up thoughts of keeping that wall around your
         heart – once you get your heart chakra activated it's
         bound to come tumbling down.

7-14   Why are you so hard on yourself? Don't you know you are
         a beautiful being worthy of not only the best treatment
         from others, but also from yourself? This means easing up
         on what I call the Three Heartbreak-Rs: Regrets, Reproach
         and Retribution.

Section 5: Throat Chakra

30-35   You're a natural leader, highly resourceful, and safe from having your boundaries plundered. People feel comfortable telling you their problems because you acknowledge them without fear or falsehood. I admire your ability to release old conditionings and speak your truth with integrity.

 15-29   There are some things you simply do have to bite your tongue about in order to keep the peace. Fair enough, as long as you're not missing out or feeling compromised. Otherwise, what exactly are you getting out of the situation?

7-14   Yes, yes, I know. You don't want to rock the boat – this would mean bringing attention to yourself, or changing the status quo. By all means, you have a choice here: continue paddling your canoe upstream, or do something about getting your throat chakra back in balance so that your needs are met.

Section 6: Third Eye Chakra

30-35   Your innate wisdom, self-assurance and clarity is such a source of comfort to your goddess sisters. You lead by example in rising above the daily bunkum, and for that, thank you for your inspiration. People often seek your advice for your unbiased viewpoints.

15-29   Are you filling your life with so much busy-ness that you don't have time to stop and count blades of grass or follow a snail's trail? Clutter is a convenient way of avoiding being with your true thoughts. Every day is a nice day for a daydream, so start escaping the toxic thought patterns from today.

7-14   It can be tempting to buy the bad-news story your ego and fear feeds you, but it's healthier to say "oh well" in the face of perceived judgement or criticism. It's none of your business what other people think of you, and it's none of your business worrying about *how* the Universe is going to deliver exactly what is right for you. Trust, and understand that everything happens at the perfect time for the perfect reason!

Section 7

30-35   La, la, la! The world is *such* a beautiful place it is worth singing and celebrating with lots of la, la, las. You have a highly-evolved sense of community and helping others achieve a better quality of life, both emotionally and spiritually. You have a spiritual nature, so let it shine ☺

15-29   You may have a faith system that sustains you, but there is enough room for doubt that you occasionally slip into more earthly concerns. It may prove very healing to record the dreams you remember and identify recurring themes running through – this could be a subliminal key to what is really going on for you.

7-14   Remind yourself, is it really the end of the world if the bins aren't emptied on time, or your home technology isn't the latest and greatest? Your challenge is to release trivial concerns – and it is all just *stuff* – in order to embrace your higher consciousness and sense of bliss.

It will be interesting to re-do the quiz once you've completed the Workout so you can see how your energies have shifted with the power of positive intention and action.

OK, so now you have a starting point of where your chakras are at right now, let's launch into the background reading about the Seven Essential Tools and Other Tools.

The Seven Major Chakras

The study of chakras dates back many centuries, and as such, they are considered an integral part of holistic health. By consciously working with your chakra energy and the issues that relate to each zone, you can bring your life into balance and experience a deep sense that all is right with your world.

In particular, you will be able to empower and uphold the seven essential facets of your life – security, abundance, power, love, truth, trust and joy.

The word chakra comes from Sanskrit (a classical language of India). The major chakras are often described as spinning wheels of light or auric energy centres. However you connect with them though, you won't find them in a physical form if you were to cut open the body – they are esoteric and vibrational energy forces that are intrinsically linked with your body and physiological wellbeing.

The seven major chakras and their life-aspect are as follows:

Base	Connection
Sacral	Abundance
Solar Plexus	Power
Heart	Love
Throat	Truth
Third Eye	Trust
Crown	Bliss

It is personal choice whether you work with the chakras from the base to the crown or vice versa. Some people bring energies into their crown and down through the meridian to the base, and then back up to the crown again. In theory, this Workout begins at the base and works up to the crown.

When all chakras are balanced and spinning at their optimum vibration level, they integrate physical, emotional, psychological and spiritual facets of the human into a coherent whole. There is generally an overlapping and sharing of functions amongst chakras, both physiologically and psychologically.

Physiological Role of Each Chakra

The base and sacral chakras are related to generative and sexual functions, while the solar plexus chakra is related to the stomach and digestion.

The heart chakra is related to the heart and circulation, and the throat chakra is related to the lungs and the voice, including the ears, nose, throat and thyroid glands.

The third eye chakra is related to vision, the eyes, and the pituitary gland, while the crown chakra is related to the brain, and especially the pituitary and pineal glands.

Psychological Role of Each Chakra

The three lower chakras are related to our raw emotions and biological instincts ranging from sexual desire and hunger, into passion, anger, pleasure and joy and other relatively simple emotional states.

The four higher chakras are related to higher cognitive states. That is, the heart chakra is related to empathy and understanding; the throat chakra is related to vocal expression, hearing, and the ability to communicate; the third eye chakra is related to clarity and the ability to understand; and the crown chakra is related to deep understanding and comprehension on a spiritual level.

Psychologically, if I become aware that a chakra is out of balance, I immediately associate it with the relevant life aspect to identify issues that need resolving or healing. For example, if my solar plexus chakra were out of balance, I'd look for signs of manipulation, disrespect, causes of anxiety, or events that disconnect me from my authentic self.

The Life Aspect, Self-Aspect, Well-Being Aspect and Vibration of Each Chakra

The major chakras influence the seven essential aspects of life that are examined in this handbook: security and connection, abundance and creativity, power, love, truth, trust and bliss.

They respond to the vibration of your thoughts and statements that begin with I have, I feel, I am (and I do), I love, I say, I see and I know.

And, they rule aspects of the inner Self that keep you balanced, well-rounded and safe: self-preservation, self-gratification, self-definition, self-appreciation, self-expression, self-reflection and self-knowledge.

Chakra	Life Aspect	Self- Aspect	Well-Being	Vibration
Base	Connection	-Preservation	Physical	I have…
Sacral	Abundance	-Gratification	Transitional	I feel…
*Hara**	Power	-Definition	Personal	I am…
Heart	Love	-Appreciation	Emotional	I love…
Throat	Truth	-Expression	Creative	I say…
*Brow**	Trust	-Reflection	Mental	I see…
Crown	Bliss	-Knowledge	Spiritual	I know…

* The hara and brow are referred to as solar plexus and third-eye chakras in this guide.

Location of Each Chakra

The chakras are located roughly near our glands along the
meridian of our body. The name of each chakra describes roughly
where it is located.

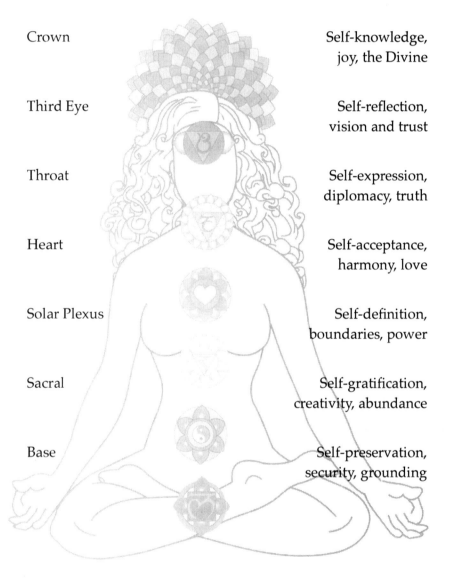

Crown	Self-knowledge, joy, the Divine
Third Eye	Self-reflection, vision and trust
Throat	Self-expression, diplomacy, truth
Heart	Self-acceptance, harmony, love
Solar Plexus	Self-definition, boundaries, power
Sacral	Self-gratification, creativity, abundance
Base	Self-preservation, security, grounding

Tools & Techniques for Balance

The 7-Day Chakra Workout is based on the daily use and implementation of many tools and approaches. The main seven tools are: essential oils, gemstones, colour, sound, archetypal goddess energy, intention and actions. Other tools include animals, earth points, flower essences, yoga and more.

When it comes to energising the chakras, we not only have a smorgasbord of tools to choose from, but also the power within to choose how we will apply them. It's a case of listening to our intuition and honouring where it leads us.

Some of the tools I suggest in this workout work as a catalyst to think bigger and further from the square than ever before – these are psychological tools, otherwise known as 'Thought Power Tools'. Other tools are tried-and-true healing methods and physiological approaches that are used by individuals and healers all over the world. Use as many or as few as you intuit is right.

The seven essential tools and auxiliary tools are as follows:

- Colours
- Essential Oils
- Gemstones
- Sound
- Archetypal Goddess
- Intention
- Actions

- Flowers
- Food
- Elements
- Directions
- The Sensory System
- Animals
- Symbols
- Mother Earth

Colours

The science of colour and how it affects our behaviour is not new, although marketing departments have only caught on in the last few decades. Think about SALE! signs and why they're always red – this colour creates a sense of urgency within us. It is also no coincidence that fast food restaurants paint their rooves bright yellow – yellow is a colour that stimulates appetite. Likewise, environmentally conscious businesses use colour schemes that are predominantly green in order to promote empathy and connection.

Natural light (which includes the seven colours of the spectrum) is required for the healthy function of human cells. By filtering natural light through your eyes stimulates your pituitary gland, which in turn releases hormones correlating with the organ of the same frequency. This is known as the science of syntonics, and forms the basis of colour therapy, or Chromotherapy.

Colours, therefore, are known to resonate with your aura and persona to heighten, lower or balance mood. Surrounding yourself with appropriate colours thereby assists you to respond to situations from an empowered space.

Colour therapy can entail the use of gemstones, candles, crystal prisms, tinted eye-glasses, coloured lights, coloured waters, art and mandalas, guided meditation, and even clothing, accessories and make-up.

The colours related to each chakra are as follows:

Base	Red	*Throat*	Light blue
Sacral	Orange	*Third Eye*	Indigo
Solar Plexus	Yellow	*Crown*	Purple
Heart	Green / Pink		

Action: Anatomy of the Colour Wheel

Sir Isaac Newton developed the first colour wheel diagram in 1666. Since then scientists and artists have studied and designed numerous variations of this concept.

In traditional colour theory, the three primary pigment colours that cannot be mixed or formed by any combination of other colours, are red, yellow and blue. When these three colours are blended, they produce secondary colours of orange, green and violet.

Colour in this wheel using only yellow, red and blue pencils to see the colours of the rainbow emerge.

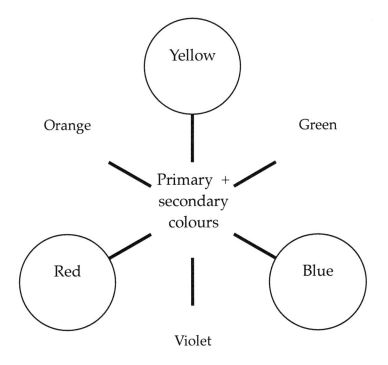

Action: Draw Down the Colours

Get into a comfortable position, close your eyes and picture a glowing white sphere above your head. Imagine the colours of the rainbow being present in the sphere, and begin.

* * *

First picture a strong red light in the sphere. Invite it down into your body, down your spine and into your base chakra. Feel your chakra flood with red as it ignites your sense of wellbeing, and gift any overflow to Gaia (Mother Earth).

Next draw the colour orange down from the sphere, along your spine and pour it into your lower abdomen. Feel your chakra brim over with orange and the light of your feminine divine glimmer and purr. Gift any overflow to Gaia.

Focussing again on the sphere, let yellow enter your body, travel down and fill your solar plexus with tigress mother energy. Gift any overflow to Gaia in the form of sunshine.

You are half-way now… draw the colour of nature from the sphere let it flow into your heart chakra. The green energy fills every corner of your heart with love and deep-seated calm. All is right in your world as you let any overflow travel through your entire body and on to Gaia.

Next, stretch your neck up draw a delicious sky blue colour into your throat˚chakra. Relax your jaw muscles as you breathe out, and gift the overflow to Gaia.

Draw down indigo next, and fill your third third eye with its properties of calm, quiet and clarity. Gift any overflow of this indigo light into the Universe.

Finally, draw down a purple or violet light and feel it pour over your crown chakra and your entire aura in a steady stream offering love, balance and protection.

Essential Oils

Certain smells can prompt memories and unlock emotions. Humans have the capability to distinguish 10,000 different smells which all affect our system in three ways – pharmacologically (interacting with the body's chemistry), physiologically (producing a stimulating or sedating effect), and psychologically (prompting emotional responses, often through memory). The process of using smells for healing is called Aromatherapy.

Aromatherapy uses essential oils and works on our sense of smell and by absorption into the bloodstream. Smells enter the nose where olfactory receptors transport them to the limbic system – the part of the brain that controls our moods, emotions, memory, instinct and learning.

Essential oils come from plants, flower, leaf, seed, bark and fruit and represent healing and living energy. They contain chemical components that can exert specific effects on the mind and body. Lavender, for example, increases alpha waves in the back of the head which promotes a sense of relaxation. Jasmine, on the other hand, increases beta waves in the front of the head, in turn promoting a more alert state.

Base	Ginger, lavender, patchouli, palmarosa, grapefruit white.
Sacral	Ylang ylang, sweet orange, grapefruit white, patchouli.
Solar Plexus	Lemongrass, eucalyptus, rosewood, peppermint, bergamot, lime, lemon myrtle.
Heart	Sweet orange, lemon, geranium, chamomile, grapefruit white, jasmine absolute.
Throat	Vetiver, cedarwood, lemon, cajeput, frankincense.
Third Eye	Cedarwood, rosemary, lavender, frankincense, lemon, basil.
Crown	Peppermint, clove, cinnamon bark, sweet orange.

Action: Create Your Own Blends

Personally I use the Goddess-ence[2] range of 100% pure blends for their transformative power. Whatever oils you choose, make sure you only use pure oils (avoid 'fragrant' oils as they are synthetic), and seek medical advice before playing with pure essential oils.

When you begin working with essential oils, start gently. You can burn each blend, for example, add a few drops to your bath, or place a bottle on your altar in the appropriate Direction.

How To Use the Goddess-ence Oils

Starting with the base chakra blend (Kali), smell each blend in order. If a particular blend is not immediately appealing, it is an indication the related chakra is out of balance – use this blend to re-energise that chakra. Work with this blend until the aroma becomes pleasant to you. You may continue using the blend to maintain that chakra's vitality on a daily or weekly basis.

Suggestions For Application

- Apply a drop onto the chakra point;
- Burn in an oil-burner or diffuser;
- Add to massage or carrier oil;
- Sprinkle into a bath;
- Infuse linen or underwear in the clothes dryer;
- Use in an atomiser and spray the room.

100% pure essential oils are suitable for oil burners, bath, foot spa, massage, linen, deodorisers, and application to energy centres and pulse points. Avoid applying oils directly to skin, and seek medical advice if you are pregnant or are prone to heart disease or skin conditions.

---

2   Goddess-ence blends are available from www.goddess.com.au

Gemstones

If it weren't for Quartz crystal we wouldn't have television, mobile phones or personal computers as we know them – these modern devices run smoothly thanks to the conductive nature of Quartz.

The ability of crystals to conduct and transform energy is becoming increasingly recognised, not only in technology, but also in terms of health applications.

Formed over eons, often at high pressure within the earth, gemstones embody intense concentrations of energy. The subsequent energetic and physical properties of gemstones resonate with different parts of the body's energy fields (depending on their origin). They also have different therapeutic properties depending on their size, shape, exact composition and even the skill of the person holding it.

Physicists tell us that all matter is simply energy in a physical form. Gemstones embody the earth's energy for a potent healing tool at a heart-felt level.

Proper selection, shaping and use of gemstones transform them into healing tools. Many healers will tell you the ideal shape for a therapeutic gem is the sphere, but if you are working with a healer whose advice you trust, go with your intuition and do what's right for you. I prefer to work with intuition and listen to which particular gemstones I am drawn to when near them.

There are many, many gem therapy protocols that have been developed (a lot of them using spheres), but you might choose to garner benefits by wearing appropriate gemstones around your neck, on your wrists, or by carrying them in your pockets.

Following is instructions for creating a gemstone wand. This can be a major project for your Chakra Workout so you will finish with a tangible reminder of the journey you have undertaken.

Typical gemstones related to each chakra are as follows:

Base	Bloodstone	*Throat*	Lapis Lazuli
Sacral	Citrine	*Third Eye*	Sodalite
Solar Plexus	Tiger Eye	*Crown*	Amethyst
Heart	Rose Quartz		

Action: Create a chakra wand with gemstones

Gemstone wands have been used for centuries in ritual and
healing, and work as a tool for focussing intention. Some wands
are very ornate with crafted wood and lashings of silver. Others
are simple using raw twigs and leather straps. How you construct
your wand is up to you, but here are some suggestions.

Prepare a shopping list based on the gemstones recommended for
each chakra. Choose a selection of gemstones consisting of two
pure Quartz stones for each tip, and seven stones representing
each of the seven chakras. Alternatively, visit a gemstone stockist
and open yourself to the appropriate gemstones presenting
themselves to you. You will also need craft tools such as a hot
glue gun, silver wire, copper wire and/or leather straps.

Select your wand by taking a walk in nature and choosing a stick
that attracts your eye, or that is gifted to you by a tree if you lean
lightly on a branch. Also collect any feathers that fall near you.
You may choose to use some sandpaper on the stick (or branch) to
polish it, or leave it raw, just as you found it.

Glue each gemstone along the length of the wand at each stage
through the Workout. That is, on Sunday glue the stone you chose
to represent the base chakra aspect of your life. On Monday, glue
the sacral chakra stone, and so on. When the seven chakra stones
have been glued on, finish the wand by gluing the quartz crystals
to either end, and tying leather straps in a decorative fashion
around the wand. Embellish the wand with your other items such
as feathers, to finish.

Sound

Our voice connects our cognitive self to the physical world. Singing, chanting and toning are three ways to get energy flowing along the chakra meridian. Likewise, sound waves coming into the body (not necessarily through your ears!) help massage your physical and auric bodies, giving you a sense of improved wellbeing.

In quantum physics we can see that our bodies are made up of atoms and electrons that are in a constant state of oscillation. When they are hit by sound waves, they resonate with the energy of each tone or shape of the sound.

The seven notes in the musical scale each correspond to a chakra. You can simply hum in each tone as required, but for the tone-deaf amongst us, there are many other ways to balance chakras via sound.

- Listen to recorded chants or Tibetan bowls in each tone, remembering to listen for the sound of silence also.

- Tuning forks are a little hit and miss at maintaining notes, but a good one can make different wavelengths.

- There's nothing like going wild on drums to release bottled up emotions, or floating on flutes to get expressive energy flowing, or pulling on the heartstrings with the violin and harp.

- Listen to a therapist's voice, or sing along to a song that helps you move emotion and energy through your body.

- Remember *Sounds of Music*? The seven musical notes of the diatonic scale are represented as sounds: do, rei, me, fa, so, la, te – as made famous in this movie.

A grooveeeee goddess friend of mine is writer, composer and performer, Casey Scott. Casey correlates the chakras to the planets: Mars, moon, sun, Venus, Mercury, Saturn and Jupiter in the order of the base to the crown.

"Johannes Kepler made correlations to tone based on the math of each planet's orbit," she explains. "It's a very elegant system which contains little three note musical phrases for each planet."

The tone of C is linked to the heart chakra and makes intuitive sense to Casey. This is because "C is the centre tone of Western music, the colour green is the centre of the visible spectrum, and the heart is the centre chakra that resides in the body."

The progression up the scale through the chakra system creates a wonderfully lifting effect, but "with most of these systems you don't necessarily get a straight ascension up the scale when plugging them into the chakra system."

"I feel pretty nerdy for knowing this stuff, but I like to feel the music I'm creating is supported by natural structures found in the heavens and the patterns of nature. That's what Bach did!"

A widely accepted theory is that "C", being a central note, forms the foundation of music and therefore relates to the base chakra:

Base	C	*Throat*	G
Sacral	D	*Third Eye*	A
Solar Plexus	E	*Crown*	B
Heart	F		

Action: Get Good Vowel-Movements

Even if you are completely and utterly tone deaf, don't worry. Steven Halpern (innerpeacemusic.com) is an artist and healer who uses music in massage, yoga and meditation. He offers a fool-proof method of toning by making extended sounds using the five vowels – a, e, i, o, u. You can sing them on just one note, on a cascade of notes, or starting low and sliding high. Steven says, "Do this five times in a row and you will experience what is known as the 'singers high'."

Archetypal Goddess

Women have many faces. In just one day, you are Ms Professional at work; partner, cook and carer at home; and Social Queen with friends. Using the ancient goddesses as role models is one way to get through each day with your integrity intact.

Modern gals can reconnect with ancient goddess energy and be inspired by their energy quite easily. Every goddess has a story of hardship and subsequent victory – just as we encounter challenges every day we can draw parallels from the goddess' stories and learn by example in order to succeed ourselves.

You can manifest goddess energy simply by being aware of yourself and making choices with intention. Every action, thought, projection of self, and treatment of others is a reflection of the goddess within.

Being 'goddess' is about channelling and showing the strengths of the real You. A modern goddess is able to tap into her intuition and trust that it guides her in the right direction. She is able to look in the mirror and say, with meaning, "I love you." And, she is able to act with integrity for her highest good at all times.

During the workout you'll be prompted with seven different goddesses each day. Apart from a brief description about each goddess' history, it's up to you to decide which one (or more) you resonate with and how much research you do to invite her energy into your life. Source her symbols, include her in your Creative Visualisation or draw her image – open your heart and she will let you know how she wishes to manifest in your life each day.

Base	Kali, Freyja, Cordelia, Gaia, Lilith, Artemis, Venus.
Sacral	Ishtar, Baubo, Ceres, Tyche, Aphrodite, Ostara, Sri Laxmi.
Solar Plexus	Pele, Astarte, Oya, Diana, Bodicea, Maia, Persephone.

Heart	Kwan Yin, Amaterasu, Hina, Tara, Hestia, Juno, Vesta.
Throat	Athena, Fortuna, Rhiannon, Dana, Demeter, Iambe, Oshun.
Third Eye	Isis, Hathor, Baba Yaga, Cerridwen, Brigid, Inanna, Epona.
Crown	Nuit, Spider Woman, Circe, Hecate, IxChel, Yemaya, Bast.

Action: Read Up

Raise your conscious goddess energy to radiate confidence, innate beauty and inspired joy – your authentic Self. Get goddess savvy and become an InnerGoddess member. Receive weekly goddess messages, affirmations and activities to help you reconnect with your inner goddess.

This is a weekly newsletter for women wishing to develop a deeper connection with their feminine divine – the place of wild yearning for more "realness" and yumminess in everyday life.

The messages are intended to help you feel beautiful, sassy and inspired as you plug back into your authentic power… the grounding force for your own inner goddess.

It should be noted that whilst we honour and revere the great mother goddess in all her forms, this is not a "how to worship the goddess" service. Rather, the messages are geared to helping you reconnect with the goddess within *you*. We draw on the goddess' stories and examine ways we can encapsulate their courageous energy, incorporate it into our own lives and learn to see ourselves as *goddess*.

www.goddess.com.au

Intention

By the time you go to bed tonight, you will have had around 60,000 thoughts go through your head. When you reflect on your day, what ratio of your thoughts were positive? Were they mostly random or deliberate? Out of left-field or in reaction to a catalyst? How lovely if 100 percent of your conscious thoughts could be positive! And even lovelier if your subconscious ones were too!

The act of being conscious and purposeful is a chakra-balancing tool called "Intention". Your intention is the act of determining mentally upon some action or result – that is, when you decide "it is to be so," then your intention will literally drive it to be so.

Your mind is a super powerful machine. Once you're in the driver's seat it's up to you how much abundance, love and joy you have in your life. When you can think positively, you can steer your intentions in a direction that proves beneficial for your highest good. Just how much you can transform your life is totally up to your imagination – literally.

Hence, I've identified three 'Thought Power Tools' that I'm focusing on for this Workout for this purpose. These tools are extremely powerful and life-changing. They complement each other so ideally work with all three at once. They are:

1.   Creative Visualisation,
2.   Affirmations and
3.   Mantras

Creative Visualisation

Where your attention goes is where your energy flows… Creative visualisation is one technique that harnesses positive thoughts to 'think' your way to an empowered future.

I was first introduced to Creative Visualisation via Shakti Gawain's book of the same name, but the practice has been around for centuries. Even Jesus referred to the power of creative thinking when he said, "Whatsoever things you desire when you pray, believe that you receive them and you shall have them."

The key word here is 'believe'. It's time to release any negative experiences in your past that have you believing you deserve hardship, obstacles and problems. Think again and believe you deserve an incredible, joyful and easy journey. Persevere with your Creative Visualisation. Even if you don't achieve your goal in one day, one week or one month, at the very least you are on the path to surmounting negative patterns.

Affirmations

Affirmations are another tool that prove very effective in changing and empowering your mindset for positive results. Basically, an affirmation is a short, positive statement that describes an ideal outcome of a wish or desire. By identifying what you want from your life and expressing it in words as though it has already come to fruition, you are sending a clear message to the Universe of what you want it to provide.

A successful affirmation has three necessary elements:

1. A Clear Sense of Purpose … The affirmation you choose must be a dedicated belief, not just an ad hoc approach to 'trying it out'. Apply your full commitment and sense of purpose to replace stale attitudes with unlimited potential.

2. Believe It … As with the Creative Visualisation, believe without fear or guilt that your desire is coming closer to fruition each time you say it. Know that you truly deserve what you are asking for, and be ready to accept it.

3. Perseverance … Work with your affirmation dozens of times daily, seven days a week, every day until your affirmation manifests as your reality. Never give up – the rewards far outweigh the effort.

This is just a suggestion, but words you can use to start each affirmation could be:

Base	I have…	Throat	I say…
Sacral	I feel…	Third Eye	I see…
Solar Plexus	I am…	Crown	I know…
Heart	I love…		

Mantras

Wikipedia.com defines a mantra as "a religious or mystical syllable or poem, typically from the Sanskrit language. They are primarily used as spiritual conduits, words or vibrations that instil one-pointed concentration in the devotee." 'Mantra' in its Sanskrit form is made up of man– ('to think') and –tra ('tool') – literally translating to an 'instrument of thought'.

Mantras are traditionally prominent in such traditions as Hinduism and Buddhism and revolve around the repetition of sound patterns such as "Om mani padme hum." The practice has evolved into modern / Western use by groups such as Transcendental Meditation practitioners. Even Christians using rosary beads for repetitive prayer is an example of a modified mantra. Personally, I like to use an affirmative word and repeat it over and over until it becomes a mantra in its function.

You can tone your mantras, incidentally, to synchronise with a relevant chakra. As outlined in *The Goddess Guide to Chakra Vitality* musical notes and sacred vowels are:

Base	LA	Throat	RE
Sacral	BA	Third Eye	AH
Solar Plexus	YM	Crown	OM
Heart	HA		

If you're tone deaf (like me), you can simply exercise your abdominal chakras by toning deeply, your heart chakra using middletones (which produces a great emotional impact on anyone listening), or the throat and upper chakras using higher tones.

Actions

It's one thing to understand the concept of chakras in your head, but another thing entirely to take the next step and do what it takes to get the job done.

There is a range of activities that you can choose to do each day to get those chakras pumping and energising your life. Do a selection of the activities, or pick just one that will fit into your lifestyle, or choose the one that your intuition tells you is the right one for you. No matter which exercise(s) you choose to do, in all cases undergo the exercise with absolute conscious energy flowing to and from the chakra you are energising.

Some physical actions you can do for each chakra include:

Base	Stomping, walking, hiking, standing, dancing.
Sacral	Shimmying, playing, eating, de-toxing.
Solar Plexus	Hula hooping, intuition development, roaring like a tiger, abdominal exercises.
Heart	Hugging, stretching, hand-over-heart meditating.
Throat	Singing, toning, speaking, journaling.
Third Eye	Studying, teaching, meditating, decision-making.
Crown	Sleeping, star-gazing, going to church / circle.

Action: Let Every Act Be Intentional

Even painting your toenails can become a sacred act if you decide to repeat (and mean) your affirmation with every stroke. Plaiting your hair is magical if you weave your creative visualisation into every twist and turn. And doodling in your journal can manifest in the most incredible mind and mood shifts if you open yourself to the energy flow that you are intending to nurture.

Other Chakra Balancing Tools

Flowers

In imagery, the chakra centres are depicted as multi-petalled flowers. Such plant life are representative of our own living forces –our energies also open to light and close to darkness. You can discover the flowers that make your soul sing by working with a Naturopath or healer on particular issues you want to resolve. If you have never self-medicated before, consult a healer to determine which flower essences to use for your situation.

Flower essence therapy was discovered back in the 1930s when British physician, Dr Edward Bach, discovered 38 flower remedies that promoted healing. He was able to sense the energetic imprints of the life force of the flowers, and their unique abilities to address emotional and mental aspects of wellness.

You can also find the best flower energy for you by listening to your intuition. Go out into your garden or a nearby park and take your pendulum (or preferred divination tool) with you. Use your intuition to guide you to flowers and plants that resonate with each of your chakras. Ask permission of each plant to gift you a flower. If you are in a national park where it is illegal to pick flowers, sketch or photograph them instead. Do not ingest the flowers unless you are absolutely certain they are safe.

Action: Associate With Flowers

When you see your flowers, see your own inner beauty matching theirs. Feel restored and free from self-imposed limitations. Know that your flowers are here to stir your creativity, inspire passion and promote visionary self-expression. That they have come from the earth will help you ground and connect with your roots.

Food

In order to achieve balanced chakras, it comes as no surprise that we need a balanced diet. After all, we are what we eat! There are different interpretations of what a balanced diet actually is, but the Healthy Eating Pyramid developed by the Australian Nutrition Foundation[3] offers a basic guide. The plan has divided foods into three groups based on each group's ability to fulfil nutritional requirements of the body. Thus, food choices are made based on nutritional properties.

On a more spiritual level, there is one school of thought that food can be divided into four main categories – foods that warm or cool, foods that increase or settle energy, foods the increase or diminish physical strength, and foods that converge or scatter sweat. Foods are selected for their nutritional properties – root plants such as ginger, leeks and carrots, for example, are used for their warming and energising gifts.

Yet another theory is that there are six basic types of nutrition. The categories are food and drink, air, sunlight, prana, earth energy and cosmic energy. All of these areas are stimulated by colour, so food choice is based on this.

And then there is the theory that there are only two food groups: natural and processed. The closer to nature that I can get my food, the better I feel about what I am putting into my body. I aim for fresh produce whenever possible, and ideally organic.

An issue that I explore in my book, *The Goddess DIET*, is that of listening to my body's signals when it comes to choosing my food – my body tells me when I'm deficient or over-indulgent by the way I handle stress, the quality of my sleep, the amount of energy I have to burn, and the length of my attention span. With some practice and trust in your intuition, you may choose to use this technique too.

---

3   www.nutritionaustralia.org

The Importance of Water

No matter what your approach is to food, a healthy body relies on plenty of water. Water is the foundation of life – more than 70 percent of the human body is water. When you're dehydrated, you feel more run-down and react more readily to stress. Avoid this by drinking the standard recommendation of eight cups of pure water every day.

Also consider your attitude to the water you drink. Japanese quantum physicist, Dr Masaru Emoto, conducted a study on the crystalline energy of water and found that a compassionate person can purify the water in his body. This in turn positively influences his life and makes him healthy.

Dr Emoto performed a series of experiments on water crystals and revealed that positive messages (such as benevolent thoughts, classical music and positive statements) purified water as evidenced by beautiful hexagonal water crystals being formed at low temperature. In contrast, water exposed to negative messages (such as bad thoughts, heavy metal music or negative characters), formed water crystals of a distorted and chaotic shape at low temperature.

Action: Get Cooking!

You will find several recipes in this Workout using ideal foods for each chakra. Scan ahead and if any particular recipes resonate with you, start your shopping list.

_____

_____

_____

_____

_____

Elements

The chakras correspond to the elements of earth, water, fire, air, sound, light and faith. Incorporating elements into your life increases your connection with nature, both on the physical plane and in the ethereal world beyond.

Each element describes the essential nature of each chakra – earth grounds us, for example; water shows us how to ebb and flow; fire transforms, air revives us, sound heals us, light inspires us and helps us see, and faith nourishes us. It is important to carry the elements in balance. Too much water can put out your spark, for example, or not enough can allow your fiery energies to rage unchecked.

The elements related to each chakra are as follows:

Base	Earth	*Throat*	Sound
Sacral	Water	*Third Eye*	Light
Solar Plexus	Fire	*Crown*	Faith
Heart	Air		

Action: Create a Sacred Elemental Space

Prepare your altar before you began the Workout – a sacred space where you can add items that symbolise your journey through this Workout. Your altar might be a table in your lounge room, or your dressing table in your bedroom – just make sure it is somewhere that you can sit or stand comfortably in front of for a few minutes each day.

There are lots of items (elemental and otherwise) listed in this Workout that you can add to your altar. I encourage you to go within and find connections with items that help you remember and reconnect with the elements at a deep and meaningful level.

Directions

Depending on where you live, the directions will have different meanings for you. For example, in the southern hemisphere, we build our homes to face North to follow the sun. Therefore, where I live at least, my North represents summer and South the winter. In the northern hemisphere, on the other hand, South equates to summer and North, winter.

It is worth noting here that this Workout is written from my perspective in the southern hemisphere.

In linking the chakras to directions, apart from North, South, East and West, the other three directions that I work with are Below, Above and Within.

When creating your altar or sacred space, you can follow the suggestions offered in this Workout (which is loosely based on the Celtic tradition), or fine-tune the process according to your intuition. Many people like to apply personal interpretations of the elements, directions and seasons according to where they live, and again, I encourage you to do the same.

The directions related to each chakra are as follows:

Base	Below	*Throat*	North
Sacral	West	*Third Eye*	Within
Solar Plexus	South	*Crown*	Above
Heart	East		

Action: Enhance Your Sacred Elemental Space

When adding items to your altar to symbolise healing or sources of strength, place each of them at a point on the altar in accordance with the relevant direction.

The Sensory System

Allow any single memory come to mind and chances are it has been indelibly imprinted with at least three sensory footprints. Smell, sound, sight, taste and touch trigger incredible emotions and memories. Scientists refer to these senses as the olfactory, gustatory, visual, somatosensory and auditory senses. There are two more senses that make up our basic seven senses. They are: our sixth sense, of empathy, intuition and insight; and our gift of Extra-Sensory Perception (also known as ESP).

Base	Smell	*Throat*	Hearing
Sacral	Taste	*Third Eye*	Sixth
Solar Plexus	Sight	*Crown*	ESP
Heart	Touch		

Animals

The power animals suggested in this Workout have come from Australia's most gifted animal shamanist, Scott Alexander King[4]. Scott has an innate gift to instinctively link the soul energy of animals with the energy of chakras.

"I invite you to trust your own feelings and develop your own correlations between the animals and your chakra system by listening to and trusting what your body tells you," he says.

You are encouraged to search for your personal power animals in this Workout. Treat the search as a ritualistic hunt for your power animal within.

Base	Bear, Koala, Duck, Praying Mantis.
Sacral	Otter, Hummingbird, Snake, Butterfly, Turtle, Cat.
Solar Plexus	Rabbit, Horse and Kangaroo for fortitude. Buffalo, Hawk and Bee for intuition.
Heart	Dog, Lady Beetle, Frog, Dove.

---

4   www.AnimalDreaming.com

Throat	Lion, Eagle.
Third Eye	Dolphin, Swan, Dragonfly.
Crown	Crow, Magpie, Unicorn, Dragon.

Action: Start Your Menagerie

Next time you're out and about, be aware which animals present themselves to you over and over again. Maybe you'll see ducks swimming in a pond, later on you'll notice them flying overhead, an illustration of a duck on a book cover will catch your eye, and the paper's headlines may scream the cricket results, "Out For a Duck!" If so, Duck could well be a significant totem animal in your life. Read about the mythology of your power animals in Scott's book, Animal Dreaming, and reflect how their message applies to you.

Action: Record Your Animal Totem Pole

One reason Native Americans create totem poles is to represent the nine different animals that act as guides and accompany each individual through life. The interesting thing is that your animal guides can come in and go out depending on the direction your life is taking, and any tasks you need to complete on your journey. It's an insightful exercise to record your animal guides on a totem along with the messages they have for you.

Symbols

Symbolism is a universal language that connects all cultures. The premise of representing chakras as symbols is to trigger growth and healing when you resonate with each allegory.

There are many different ways to depict chakra energy in a visual format. Symbols that illustrate chakras can include multi-petalled flowers, Sanskrit shapes, or planetary profiles (to name just a few). Basic symbols however, begin with the following:

Base	Square	*Throat*	Circle
Sacral	Pyramid	*Third Eye*	Star
Solar Plexus	Cross	*Crown*	Lotus
Heart	Chalice		

Action: Create a 7-Pointed Mandala

You will need to dig out your high-school maths equipment for this. Find your old compass, protractor, ruler (hopefully it will still have "I ♥ Matt Dillon" etched into it so that you may enjoy many happy memories!) and coloured pencils.

Draw a circle with your compass. Every circle has 360°, so divide 360 by 7. You should get 51.4°.

Use your protractor to mark seven points in the circle at 51.4° apart from each other. Pencil a line from Point 1 to 2 to 3 and so on, until you end up with a heptagon.

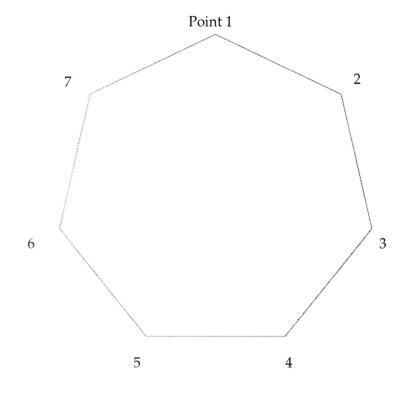

Starting at Point 1, rule a line to across the circle to Point 3, then across to Point 5, 7, 2, 4, 6 and back to 1. You should end up with a seven-pointed star (heptagram).

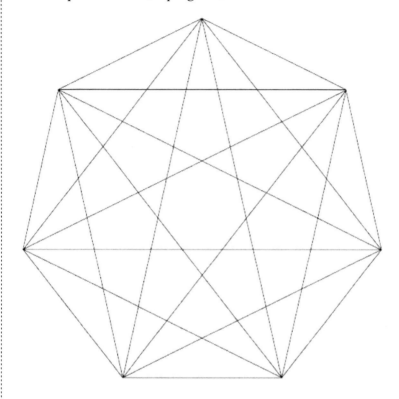

Unleash your creative diva and colour your mandala. Use affirmations and mantra with each colour you use.

Can you see the acute ⁂ and obtuse ⬡ shapes inside this diagram? Which shape suits your purpose for this mandala?

The acute heptagram, for example, is also called an Elven Star or Faery Star and is sacred to those who follow the Faery tradition and Otherkin subculture. The obtuse heptagram is used by many cultures, including the Hindus in the chakra system, and us Australians on our national flag.

Mother Earth

A man by the name of Hamish Miller[5] used his dowsing rods in an effort to explain the earth's energy fields on human behaviour. He discovered the now famous Mary and Michael lines that link many sacred sites, from St Michael's Mount in Cornwall, through to Glastonbury and many other sacred sites. These ley lines form part of Mother Earth's sacred geometry – a geometric blueprint of naturally occurring patterns and rhythms that form our physical reality.

As a living organism, Gaia (Mother Earth), has chakra points linked with grid points around the world, all of which are based on these laws of sacred geometry. Archaeologists, alchemists, anthropologists, historians and geometricians use these myths, metaphors and mathematics to explain the relationships between our natural world and how that affects our chakras.

There are many theories about where the earth's chakras are, but ultimately the most influential chakra points are those that resonate with you personally.

One theory is being documented by a group of pilgrims in Glastonbury. Members of the Rainbow Serpent Tribe[6] are making a feature film of their journey to seven points on the planet that they believe are home to chakra energy.

Tor Webster is the director of the project, and says the groups intends to document the communities who live on each of the earth chakras, as well as follow the two great energy currents that traverse the planet, commonly known as the female Rainbow Serpent and the male Plumed Serpent.

---

5   Miller H, Broadhurst P, The Sun and the Serpent, Pendagron Press, 1990. ISBN 978-0951518311. (Order the book online at http://snipurl.com/leylines)

6   www.RainbowSerpent.co.uk

When I asked Tor why particular locations have been selected as the chakra points, he replied, "This is the reason of the Rainbow Serpent Project – to explore this and find out. Maybe by balancing the earth chakras through coming together creating ceremonies, communicating and celebrating we can create a unity and oneness which will help with the unrest of this planet."

The locations that Tor is exploring in his documentary are:

Base	Mount Shasta, California.
Sacral	Lake Titicaca, South America.
Solar Plexus	Uluru, Australia.
Heart	Glastonbury, England.
Throat	The Great Pyramid of Giza, Mount Sinai and the Mount of Olives.
Third Eye	Glastonbury (but for you, the earth chakra point is wherever your intuition says it is).
Crown	Mount Kailas, Tibet.

Action: Connect With Mother Earth

That there are so many theories gives you permission to explore each one and work out which one (if any!) resonates with you. Take time to reflect on Mother Earth's organic and logarithmic curves so you'll be able to establish your own chakra-based relationship with her.

Using the Tools in Your 7-Day Workout

As I mentioned earlier, you have the power to choose which tools you will use and how you will apply them. In this chapter you will have immediately felt drawn to try some tools more than others. Make a note of these tools and aim to have them on hand before you start the workout.

_____

_____

_____

_____

_____

_____

_____

_____

_____

_____

_____

_____

_____

_____

The next chapter details more specifically at each of the chakras, their life aspect, the domain of Self- which they rule, their main theme, their location in the body and physical manifestation of balance and imbalance. We'll also look at which tools resonate with each chakra.

Base Chakra :: Sunday

The base chakra connects us with the physical plane. It fires our survival instincts, grounds us and forms the basis of our security, whether that security be in terms of employment, income, moral or physiological, family-based or health related.

Sunday is the first day of the week, and named in honour of the sun – the centre of our Solar system, source of light and sustainer of life. Just as the planets revolve around the sun, your base chakra is a virtual anchor to all the aspects of your life.

Positive Traits

Perseverance, willpower, discipline and authority – all aspects of masculine sun energy. Other traits include confidence and the will to live and thrive.

Another aspect is that of earth mother. With love as her driving force, she is the nurturer who forms a deep connection with her family. She loves nature, her self, the community and the planet. Basic needs are paramount, as is the sustainability of resources to meet those needs.

People who have highly charged base chakras make good athletes, fire fighters, police officers and builders. They tend to be always on the move, very trustworthy, and like their facts presented as black and white. There are no grey areas in their search for truth and justice.

When Out of Balance…

Negative tendencies can include excessive control issues, fear of being alone, inhibition, an attitude of defeat, immobility, indecisiveness and isolation. These tendencies can occur in situations where security is threatened, especially when the catalyst is out of your control such as losing a loved one, getting fired from your job or being evicted from your home.

Symptoms of an imbalanced base chakra include confusion, irrational outbursts of anger, inexplicable dissatisfaction with life or feelings of suppressed frustration. Maybe you're feeling stuck in a rut. Or perhaps even you're wondering how the heck you ended up with the life you are living. If you are feeling unsettled or that you are at a crossroads, consciously focus on energising your base chakra (and thereby your security and sense of intention).

As Part of Your Life Journey

The base chakra is affected by your infancy stage. Any traumas experienced within the family unit are housed in this chakra and can manifest later in life as poor health, sexual addiction or repulsion, a sense of restlessness or a need to be in control. Disturbances in the security of the family unit such as moving house, loss of a sibling or the absence or loss of a parent through divorce or death, can result in core issues around your beliefs.

Sex addicts and control freaks are an extreme result of abuse during this time. If your approach to life is 'my way or the highway', check the degree of confrontation in your attitude. Be honest with yourself – are you masking an innate feeling of weakness, or a lack of trust in others? A stable and loving infancy, however, instils a sense of security in the family unit, trust in relationships and a core ability to receive support.

Tools for the Base Chakra

Colour

Red. Red is the colour of fire, blood and the pulsating heart beating with passion. This colour is often the chosen as a favourite by extroverts for its implied energy. It increases your heart and respiration rate, your metabolism and your blood pressure – it's no wonder then that you 'see red' when you are highly charged with emotion.

Essential Oils

Ginger to boost self-confidence, lavender, patchouli and palmarosa for their calming properties, and grapefruit white to energise and uplift willpower. Keep a bottle in your underwear drawer – the aroma will infuse into your underwear which is then worn right next to my base chakra. If you're in upheaval at work at the time of doing this Workout (perhaps you are vying for a promotion, or there are redundancies in the wind), sprinkling a few drops onto your office chair will help you feel more settled.

Gemstones

Healers use Hematite to treat blood-related illnesses; choose Garnet to balance libido, aid commitment and in a crisis. Tourmaline grounds spiritual energy and brings protection, as does Ruby. In addition, Ruby helps you connect more deeply with your heart chakra energies while you are working with life aspects of movement and motivation. Bloodstone (a green quartz with flecks of red jasper) offers complementary colours that give an active balance of yin/yang, calm/vigour; and Smoky Quartz fortifies resolve and allows passion to flow.

Sound

Play bowls and bells in the tone of C, hum the mantra 'lam' or the vowel 'e' as in red. Stomp in time to earthenware drums. If you'd prefer to dance to some music, go for soul, gospel and anything with a fat base guitar. Sing songs about family, home, success and finding your way, or write your own songs using the base cello or base guitar.

Archetypal Goddess

Being earth goddess is about being in tune with your physical body, and being able to respond to threatening situations rationally and calmly. It also means giving back to Mother Earth her nurturing in equal measure. Role models include Kali, Freja, Cordelia, Gaia, Lilith, Artemis, Venus.

Intention

Key words and themes to incorporate into your visualisation, affirmation or mantra can revolve around feeling safe on your journey. Themes for release include insecurity, invisibility, boredom, disconnection from humanity or impatience.

Sense

Smell. Right from the time you were an itty-bitty baby, your sense of smell is your most primitive sense. It is the first sense that was activated after your birth, and you have been storing emotional connections with smells ever since. When we smell these things we are instantly carried away to places where we feel safe, and we think of people who we feel safe with. Certain smells trigger our fight or flight mechanism, or alert us that action is required. We know it is not safe to cook foodstuffs if they smell 'off'. The waft of gas in the air alerts us to a leak, preventing a potential fire. These are all essential skills in the pursuit of self-preservation.

Flowers

Flower essences include Red Chestnut, Mimulus, Aspen, Holly, Red Clover, Honeysuckle, Clematis, Cherry Plum. Flower essences aside, add\ a display of red flowers to your environment. Red carnations (admiration), poppies (pleasure), and roses (love). Gift this bouquet to yourself for your office desk, kitchen table or your altar.

Food

Enjoy red fruits such as raspberries, strawberries, cherries and tomatoes throughout the day. Root vegetables to include on your menu include carrots, potatoes, parsnips, radishes, beetroot, onions and garlic. Other foods to enjoy include red capsicum, red meat and, for the sake of anti-oxidants (!) red wine. You can also include protein rich foods such as eggs, beans, tofu and peanut butter. Of particular interest when working with grounding, is the root herb, ginger.

Element

Earth. The grounding properties of Mother Earth represent our fundamental bond to family and home. She is a symbol of sustenance, fruitfulness, solidity and endurance. And she connects each and every human being on this planet uniting us as a collective community and extended family. Not enough earth element in your environment can lead you to feel flighty, while too much can bog you down. In the appropriate Direction, place symbols of soil, plants, twigs and stones onto your altar.

Direction

Below. Underlying our every thought and action, is the primal instincts and conditioning of our youth. When the maiden goddess Persephone travelled below to the Underworld she met and befriended her shadow side to become the Queen of Darkness. In other words, in facing adversity she discovered her true personal power. Consider hibernating for a little while and meeting aspects of yourself that have been long-buried in the face of contemporary social conditioning. Add a symbol to your altar that represents a secret you are harbouring, or a shadow side that you are hiding. Assemble this item next to (or below!) the item you have chosen to represent the element of Earth.

Animals

For Scott Alexander King the animal guardians associated with the base chakra are those best described as earthy, grounded and stable. They exude a sense of equilibrium, balance and inner knowing. They include Bear, Koala, Duck, Praying Mantis.

Symbols

Considering the base chakra is about your foundation and grounding, it's not surprising that many symbols are based on the building block of the square. Other interpretations of the base chakra manifest with elements such as four petals, a downward pointing triangle, a coiled kundalini or snake, an elephant, or other symbols that represent Earth.

Four gives honesty, foundation, masculine will, feminine kundalini and fertility. It indicates a square deal – sincere, achievable and deliverable. Four walls in a home equates to security and family. And this shape happily encompasses the four corners of the earth.

Mother Earth

Mount Shasta is located about 100 kilometres south of the California-Oregon border. Native Americans, who have inhabited the area for over 9,000 years, considered it the centre of creation. Their belief was that the Great Spirit used the summit as a stepping-stone from heaven to earth, whereupon he created rivers, trees and animals.

Mount Shasta also represented a territorial boundary for the Shasta, Modoc, Wintu and Ajumawi/Atsuwegi tribes. Hence, this is a place of origin, foundation, constitution and new beginnings. It is an initiation point for those embarking on a journey of meditation and discovery.

Sacral Chakra :: Monday

The sacral chakra is the seat of our shifting moods and emotions. Optimists and free thinkers are able to utilise these fluctuating energies and live life to the full. They are able to make meaningful friendships with others through creativity, emotional tolerance and sexuality. Creativity and productiveness is heightened when this chakra is awakened. Balancing your sacral chakra enables you to accept responsibility for your own choices and desires, accept change gracefully, release anxieties and past hurts, and take opportunities to let the depth of your feelings show.

The correlation between Monday's namesake, the moon and women is intrinsically linked. Feminine cycles reflect the moon's journey, just as cycles ebb and flow through the phases of new, emerging, full and waning energies. It is consequently the seat of our shifting moods and emotions.

Positive Traits

Positive aspects of the sacral chakra include creativity, abundance and sensuality. This chakra brings us fluidity and grace, depth of feeling, sexual fulfilment, and the ability to accept change. Optimists and free thinkers utilise these fluctuating energies and live life to the full. They are able to make meaningful friendships with others through creativity, emotional tolerance and sexuality.

When Out of Balance…

The changeable aspect of the moon is mirrored through our emotions. The sacral chakra, therefore, can go out of balance if you denigrate your femininity or retain stress rather than ride with your moods. You know you are out of balance if you are feeling there is no joy in life. You might be quick to show impatience, you're feeling scattered and you're exhausted – probably from trying to chase fun. Furthermore, poor body image or self-criticism manifests as depression, anorexia, bulimia or alcoholism.

When your sacral chakra is out of balance there is often an element of shallowness in your dealings with others, and a degree of irresponsibility in your behaviour. Perhaps the biggest giveaways of an imbalance are promiscuity, a creative block, financial hardship (or a poverty consciousness), or the loss of interest in love-making.

The Sacral Chakra as Part of Your Life Journey

This chakra is linked to your childhood, from the time you left the comfort of your mother's bosom to build confidence in your own abilities. Many core beliefs are instilled in children at this age, where they are retained in the sacral chakra until adulthood. A spoiled child becomes a demanding adult who is prone to addictions, for example. Or a child who has had negative comments about their weight develops eating disorders.

A child who has been allowed to play and laugh, on the other hand, is better equipped to look on the bright side of life later on. Give children the freedom to explore and express their feelings and they are more likely to be fun-loving, carefree, spontaneous and playful optimists later in life. They are better equipped to make friendships in the long term.

Tools for the Sacral Chakra

Colour

Orange. This colour stimulates the appetite – not just for food, but also for joy and wisdom. It combines the passionate energy of red and the cheerfulness of yellow. The redder the hue, the more it implies sexual desire and a thirst for action or ambition. The more golden the hue, the greater the prestige and abundance. Use orange when you want to become more enthusiastic and active about a project; to increase creative urges and flow; to spice things up if you're in a rut; and as relief from getting too serious about life.

Essential Oils

Ylang ylang is used for its anti-depressant qualities. To reach the centre of your creativity and personal power, sweet orange is used along with grapefruit white to relieve anxiety and patchouli for its calming effect. An ideal time to burn this blend is during a belly-dancing or yoga class, or while you're getting dressed and affirming your reflection in the mirror.

Gemstones

Orange gemstones are great facilitators for accepting change, improving self-esteem and stimulating creativity. These can be carried in your jeans pockets against your sacral chakra. Commonly found on beaches, Carnelian restores vitality and promotes trust in nature's cycles. Also Citrine or Brown Jasper.

Sound

Swirl and swing your hips in time to hypnotic trances and belly-dancing music. Listen to music or play crystal bowls in the tone of D, hum the mantra 'vam' or the vowel 'o' as in home. Chant the sacred vowel, BA. Sing songs about being empowered, freedom, celebrating womanhood, revellion and acceptance of life moving on. Write songs using an instrument such as the tuba.

Archetypal Goddess

The sacral chakra goddesses rule over the domains of self gratification, creativity, abundance and the feminine divine. Goddesses such as Ishtar, Baubo, Ceres, Tyche, Aphrodite, Ostara and Sri Laxmi show us how to creatively, emotionally and sexually, connect with others through feeling, desire, sensation and movement. We can learn to accept change gracefully, release anxieties and past hurts. Belly dancers are the ultimate example of women with super charged sacral chakras. They adore their feminine form and thus have a healthy attitude towards body image and self. They are literally, the embodiment of the feminine divine.

Intention

Key words and themes to incorporate into your sacral chakra affirmation can revolve around fun, play, sexuality, joy, femininity, freedom, flow, trust, permission, abundance, prosperity and creativity. Themes for release include control, fear, prudishness, self-loathing, self-judgement, creative block and depression.

Sense

Taste. The sense of taste gives us the enjoyment of food. It also drives our appetite by telling us we like the taste of sugar when we need carbohydrates, salt when we need more sodium chloride in our diet, and so on. Functionality aside, taste is a very emotional experience. We may eat to survive, but more often than not we also eat for comfort, out of boredom, or for the sheer delight of it. Eating is a very social thing to do. We meet friends for coffee, we go on dinner dates, we have breakfast meetings, we eat as a family. Even cooking is an act of love. Take every opportunity to relish your food. Let it titillate your sense of taste and ignite your sense of creative fire.

Flowers

Flower remedies for depression, self-pity and hope include Mustard, Gorse, Gentian, Sweet Chestnut, Willow. The little yellow flowers of the Evening Primrose are used to relieve hormone-induced symptoms in Pre-Menstrual Tension and menopause. Also, Poppy and Pomegranate. Apart from essences, orange blossom, Gerberas, Lantana, Marigolds and Nasturtium.

Food

Naturally, we start with the obvious 'orange' fruit and vegetables – oranges, tangerines, capsicum, carrots, pumpkin, peaches, apricots, mangos, passionfruit and rockmelon. In animal products we have egg yolks and honey. And then we have foods that simply relax us and help us feel pampered and happy. Foods that appeal to the senses are called organoleptic, and chocolate is definitely on this list. Some would even say chocolate is proof that the goddess loves us as is it such a great mood enhancer – it contains a double whammy of stimulants in antioxidants and methylxanthines. For a healthier snack, try nuts such as almonds, walnuts and pistachios. Or, if you're focussing on cleansing your lower intestinal tract, you may choose to fast lightly or go through a mini detox with herbal teas and lots of water.

Element

Water. Emotions are constantly on the move – ebbing and flowing, bubbling along happily or freezing over. As emotions and the ability to accept change correspond with the sacral chakra, the link to water is deep. Water is unique in that it can take the shape and character of its surrounds. It can be passive or stormy, stagnant or running, clear or murky, fresh or salty, fluid or solid. No matter what the form, we are drawn to all its forms at some time or another. Drinking two litres a day is essential for our survival, yet too much can be as destructive as a tsunami. Enjoy the invigoration of baths and hot showers, swimming in a lake or the ocean, or even jumping in puddles, but don't get so emotional that you dampen your spirit. Add a fish bowl, vase, floating flowers or other symbols of water to your altar.

Direction

West. West is about the setting sun and the ebbing energies of autumn. As such, West represents completion, realisation, forgiveness, emotional balance and a sense of arrival. "All is well," you might say as you watch a setting sun – the same feeling is invoked when calling in energies of the West (also the element of water in Celtic tradition.) Understand that you are bringing about deep transformation and healing through introspection and your intention for positive change. Colours to include on your altar include the autumnal range of reds, oranges and yellows. A symbol of abundance such as a cornucopia or coins are also appropriate additions.

Animals

The animal embodiments of the sacral chakra must be sinuous, liberated (on all levels) and peaceful. They should represent the balancing force that keeps the boiling pot of conception healthy and productive; the inner cauldron that resides inherently within each of us that, when celebrated, simmers and bubbles bringing joy and fertility to all areas of our life. Scott loves Otter, Hummingbird, Snake, Butterfly, Turtle and Cat for this purpose.

Symbols

The sacral chakra is orange and generally has six lotus petals. In numerology, six represents finding balance within your environment – light and dark, wild and domestic, inside and out. Sometimes the sacral chakra is symbolised with a crescent moon in the centre. The moon, of course, governs the ebb and flow of tides and the biological cycles in women. The yin-yang symbol is also applicable for the eternal flow of equal and opposite, male and female, wild and calm energies it represents. If you include this in your own creation, you are consciously aiming to release control of your emotions in order to let them flow.

Mother Earth

Lake Titicaca is the highest lake in the world, residing between the Bolivia-Peru border in the Andes Mountains in South America. There are many islands in the lake, one of which is the Island of the Sun (Isla del Sol). The Rainbow Serpent and the Plumed Serpent cross paths here, and in harmony with Andean legend, represent the male and female energies needed for conception and birth.

Solar Plexus Chakra :: Tuesday

The solar plexus chakra is known as the power chakra. It rules our personal power, fear, autonomy and metabolism. When balanced, this chakra brings us energy, effectiveness, spontaneity, and a healthy sense of Self.

This chakra resonates with the planet Mars, after which Tuesday is named. Being the planet representing war and conflict, it took on the male energy of the Roman god of war, Mars. Tuesday, therefore, is the perfect day to think about all things associated with courage, action, initiative and daring.

Positive Traits

When the solar plexus chakra is spinning at its optimum level, it is easy to feel invincible as the life of the party and a magnet to success, good luck and fantastic opportunities. It helps you feel positive about your skills and abilities, optimistic in the way you can apply them, and supports your intuitive decision-making.

Depending on your personality type, a healthy solar plexus chakra can give you the courage to be outgoing, self-assertive and confident in your self-expression. Generally motivated by success, these pioneering tendencies make for great entrepreneurs, salespeople and CEOs.

For the more introverted amongst us, a balanced solar plexus chakra gives us a greater sense of self-sufficiency, empowerment when working alone, quiet self-confidence and trustworthiness, and the ability to prioritise what is really important in life. These people make great computer technicians, engineers, researchers or psychologists.

When Out of Balance...

If you're an extrovert your solar plexus chakra is out of balance when you live according to what you do, rather than who you are. You also tend to pigeon-hole others according to what they do. In this case, you are probably the person who goes to parties and opens conversations with, "what do you do for a living?"

The negative aspect of this is that you will struggle if your cause is taken away from you because you don't have that to define you any longer. Or, if you are neck-deep in a project, it is easy to let this project get in the way of the more important cause of being true to yourself. This can lead to a sense of loss, a quick temper or impulsive actions that compensate for a feeling of uselessness.

If you're an introvert, on the other hand, you may be feeling manipulated or ignored when this chakra is out of balance. This manifests as a sense of victimisation or of being bullied, which in turn manifests as reduced self-confidence and indecisiveness.

The Solar Plexus Chakra as Part of Your Life Journey

Between the ages of 14 to 21, we develop our identity in the world – we learn boundaries at this critical time in our self-development. If you were laughed at or ridiculed or bullied at school, you may have self-esteem and confidence issues. As such, you don't like crowds, life might seem overwhelming, or you have been described as over-sensitive. Fear of rejection (stemming from a sense of unworthiness) plays a prominent role in your relationships. Unfulfilled yearnings for love experienced as an adolescent may result in a feeling of emptiness as an adult. This emptiness can manifest in you becoming a career over-achiever or a chronic under-achiever – that is, you either strive to be the super-star at work for the recognition and kudos it will bring you, or you tell yourself your menial role is all you deserve.

Tools for the Solar Plexus Chakra

Colour

Yellow. Bright yellow is the cheerful colour of sunshine, happiness, sassy energy and joy. It can cause us to salivate and our tummies to growl with anticipation of food. Its attention-grabbing nature stimulates mental activity and muscle energy.

It links our left-brain reasoning processes with our intuition, otherwise known as 'gut instinct'. Some doctors paint their rooms bright yellow to promote happiness and relieve depression, yet rooms dominated by this colour are known to make babies cry more. Use yellow to improve digestion and appetite, and to bring some sunshine on cloudy days.

Essential Oils

Lemongrass and eucalyptus cleanse and decongest the chakra ready for the energies of rosewood, (used for its restorative qualities), peppermint to promote a pleasant sense of stimulation, bergamot to uplift, and lime and lemon myrtle to promote clarity and assertiveness. This blend works very well in conjunction with the third eye chakra blend to promote trust in your intuition – use the blends to better read your gut reaction to situations.

Gemstones

Carry or wear yellow gemstones to promote your unique style and sense of self. They help your ability to listen to your intuition and innate wisdom, enhance decision-making skills, and assist with the digestive process. Tiger Eye reminds me on a conscious level to be my own tigress mother – it's amazing how this consciousness helps me stand up for myself in stressful situations. Esoterically it also brings integrity and empowers intention. Amber, (actually a fossil tree resin), Yellow Jade, Iron Pyrites, Citrine, and Rhodochrosite.

Sound

Sing aloud to any song that seems to describe who you are or who you want to be. Play crystal or Tibetan bowls in the tone of E, hum the mantra 'yam' or the vowel 'a' as in heart. Chant the sacred vowel of YM. Fill your belly with breath and intention, and belt out some songs that rally your sense of self-worth and remind you who you were born to be.

Archetypal Goddess

Solar plexus chakra goddesses rule the domain of Self Ownership – you (and only you) are responsible for your own actions, how you react to others, and for the Self that you present to the world. These goddesses encourage you to delve deeper than the superficial exterior that we have been conditioned to develop. Work out who you are, who you want to be, and then present this True You to everyone you meet. Pele, Astarte, Oya, Diana, Bodicea, Maia and Persephone will boost your personal power.

Intention

Anchor key words and themes around reclaiming power, keeping power and being empowered. Also look at integrity, authenticity, respect and self-worth. Themes for release include manipulation, bullying, anxiety, fear and self-loathing.

Sense

Sight. Your vision is your *physical* means of assessing your world. Your solar plexus chakra is the seat of your *intuitive* perception of your world. Your intuitive sight takes what you see physically and translates that information into body wisdom.

Flowers

Sunflower and Dandelion essences for youth, joy, resilient strength, and improved appetite and digestion. Other essences include Daffodil, Larch, Wild Rose, Gentian, Crab Apple, Vine, Elm, Centaury, Cerato, Scleranthus. Yellow flowers sing happiness and self-confidence.

Food

Stress is often harboured in the solar plexus chakra – you may get a knot in your stomach, or you can have a 'gut-full' of a situation. Certain foods can assist in alleviating such stress. Carbohydrates, for example, help provide the extra energy you require to sustain you through stressful times. They also help regenerate the feel-good hormone, serotonin, which otherwise drops during periods of stress. To prevent your energy levels rising and dipping dramatically, however, it is important to eat the right kind of carbohydrates. Avoid simple carbohydrates (refined sugar, white bread, white rice and so forth) and aim for high-fibre complex carbohydrates such as beans. Beans replenish your supply of Vitamin B6 – another manufacturer of serotonin. Wholemeal pasta is a good complex carbohydrate to eat today; cheese is a good protein; and cook with real butter. Also abstain from alcohol – it is filtered through the liver and spleen and adds to your body's stress levels. Yellow fruits, vegetables and seeds such as lemons, grapefruit, bananas, pineapple, corn, yellow capsicum and sunflower seeds. Herbs such as turmeric, cumin and fennel will add a yellow theme to your meals. For in between meals, chamomile tea – it promotes a sense of wellbeing and calm.

Element

Fire. The expression, 'fire in my belly', describes feelings of passion and determination. We depend on fire for warmth, cooking and even protection, yet left unchecked it can rage out of control. Its ability to transform metals to jewellery represents our ability to transform ourselves from conditioned beings to healthy beings. Its symbolism includes the sun, the Olympic flame and the hearth's home fires. Add candles, matches and a cauldron to your altar.

Direction

South. South is associated with winter in the southern hemisphere. The energy resonates with midnight, mystery, enchantment and groundedness. We are able to see things with greater clarity and begin to understand our path from childhood to now, and how our experiences have crafted our natures. We can heal, release negative conditioning, restore innocence and trust, and become reacquainted with our Self. For you altar, pine needles and cones are two symbols of winter, as are snow domes, ski gear, winter woollies, hats and scarves, plants such as holly and poinsettias (reminiscent of a northern winter) and animals that hibernate in the winter. An image of a snow-laden wilderness, a photo of yourself skiing, or even a feather from your doona to represent the act of snuggling down.

Animals

Animals exemplifying the essence of the naval chakra must offer fortitude and motivation. They must be able to lift us out of the mundane and offer us a sense of direction and purpose. Fortitude: Rabbit, Horse, Kangaroo. Intuition: Buffalo, Hawk, Bee.

Symbols

This chakra is often represented with 10 petals along with an inverted triangle. In numerology, the number 10 is reduced to the number 1, representing new beginnings, achieving goals, taking action, courage, originality, independence, and self-reliance. The three-sides of the triangle also represent your personal trinity. St Paul's trinity is 'faith, hope and love'. My trinity is 'love, truth and passion'. A friend's trinity is 'love, wisdom and power'. Decide what three words or symbols represent *you*.

Mother Earth

Uluru, Australia. The roaming film-maker, Tor Webster, feels that the geometric centre of the solar plexus earth chakra is equidistant between Uluru and the Olgas in the Uluru-Kata Tjuta National Park in Australia's Northern Territory – the place where the Rainbow Serpent begins and ends his journey around the earth. Focus on a personal connection with Mother Earth. Take responsibility for the ongoing care and revitalisation of her, whether that be by physical or ethereal means.

Heart Chakra :: Wednesday

Most of us now understand that we are motivated by two things only – fear or love. Our heart chakra, therefore, rules how we give and receive the greatest force in the Universe – love. When you stop to consider this, it is possible to understand how vital a role this chakra plays in our overall happiness.

The heart chakra is related to love and is the balance of opposites in the psyche: mind and body, yin and yang, and the upper and lower chakras. Likewise, Wednesday is the middle of the week. It is named after Mercury which rules over intellect, versatility, healing and mediation.

Positive Traits

A healthy fourth chakra promotes enhanced empathetic abilities and facilitates meaningful connections with others. Here we find our capacity for gratitude, generosity, warmth and balance. A functioning heart chakra also allows us to love deeply, feel compassion and enjoy a deep sense of peace and harmony.

If you're the type who can make friends easily, find joy in a child's giggle or the hues of a sunset, and can express yourself easily through laughter and tears, your heart chakra is in a beautiful position. You would make a great counsellor, caregiver (nursing or childcare), healer or wedding planner.

When Out of Balance...

Trust issues, betrayals, rejections, self-criticism or perceived wrongs are a result of your heart chakra being out of balance. These manifest as possessiveness, excessive sentimentality, thoughts of retribution, fear of trust, and guilt. It can also mean you prefer to live vicariously through others rather than feel the thrill of living for yourself.

When your heart chakra is out of balance, it becomes difficult to express your heart's desire. You might be harbouring guilt or grief, or maybe you have a lack of trust in others (or your Self!) To counter these feelings it is natural instinct to build a wall around your heart – this might stop others coming in to hurt you, but it also prevents you from reaching out to those who can help.

If you find it difficult to connect with others in a meaningful way, energise your heart chakra to promote more honest connections. Above all, learn to accept and love yourself unconditionally in order to attract the deep love you deserve from others.

The Heart Chakra as Part of Your Life Journey

It is interesting that the heart chakra corresponds physically with the thymus gland. Study is still being conducted on this gland, but what is known is that as we grow older the gland atrophies from about the age of 20 – a time when we are growing away from our parents' nest and learning boundaries for new relationships. From 21 to 28 years of age, one becomes more aware your life actions and taking more responsibility for your destiny.

Tools for the Heart Chakra

Colour

Green and / or *Pink*. Green positively stimulates the heart chakra. It is the colour of nature, healing, growth, safety and new beginnings. Being a restful colour, it helps those suffering from depression or nervousness and promotes a willingness to love and connect. As change and transformation are necessary properties for growth, green is a great colour to facilitate positive change. Green energy is prevalent in other areas too – the green olive branch is representative of peace, the green traffic light conveys safety, and greens heading towards the aqua spectrum bring great joy and energy. Add more green to your life to promote growth, balance, and to harness nature's life force, and this is how it will manifest for you.

Pink is another colour associated with the heart chakra. It is the colour of Universal love. The blending of red (potential) and white (purity) creates a range of pink energies. Magenta helps you stand firm against disorder and pain; crimson raises passionate energy; soft pink increases tenderness, love and acceptance. Use pink to promote love, learn how to accept help, find new levels of calmness, and break down the wall that hides your gorgeous soul.

Essential Oils

Sweet orange to reduce anxiety. This clears the way for lemon (clarity), geranium and chamomile for balancing mood swings, grapefruit white to stimulate energy flows, and jasmine absolute – an aphrodisiac that brings optimism and balance. A couple of drops on a pad inside an aromatherapy pendant is a gorgeous way to wear this blend close to your heart.

Gemstones

Green gemstones promote prosperity, balance and fertility, while pink stones promote love, self-worth and trust. Wear heart stones on a long chain so they rest near your heart. Rose Quartz, Green Tourmaline, Emerald, Green Aventurine, Malachite, Peridot, Kunzite, Rhodonite.

Sound

Hug yourself, hold hands with loved ones, and close your eyes in gratitude as you listen to any heart tones and songs. Listen to any song that pulls on the heartstrings – especially those played by stringed instruments. Inspiring love songs help open you to possibilities, and sing-alongs with friends break down walls. Play instruments in the tone of F, and chant the sacred vowel of HA.

Archetypal Goddess

The modern goddess gal never, ever allows herself to accept second best. Consider that if you don't love yourself, you can't expect others to either. Furthermore, if you let others treat you badly, you are telling your authentic self that you do not deserve better. Heart chakra goddesses such as Kwan Yin, Amaterasu, Hina, Tara, Hestia, Juno and Vesta teach us how to rally our self-love and respect, and to then mirror this energy back to others.

Intention

The one underlying theme for heart chakra affirmations is rooted in the Universe's greatest power: love. All other key words build on this theme: compassion, joy, trust, empathy, balance and harmony. Themes for release include distrust, guilt, grief, intolerance, resentment, self-loathing and bitterness.

Sense

Touch. Touch is a vital ingredient in the emotional, biological, communicative, psychological and social development of humans. As babies we were breast-fed, nursed, burped, carried or worn in slings. Mothers cuddled us, dressed us, held us by the hand, and kissed us often. These forms of non-verbal communication taught us about empathy, trust, acknowledgement, tolerance and connection with others – all domains of the heart chakra. Touch teaches us about detachment, attachment, fear, anger and playfulness, and all without saying word. Without it, both children and animals develop very slowly and even die. Researchers at the Touch Research Institute at the University of Miami, reported a 47 percent weight gain in premature babies who were massaged for 15 minutes, three times a day for 10 days. That's love in action.

Flowers

The art of honest relationships with self and others, and the act of sincere connections with those in your world, resides in your heart chakra. For Connection: Water Violet, Star of Bethlehem. Compassion: Beech, Heather. The 3 Heart Break-R's (Regrets, Reproach and Retribution): Pine, Willow, Sweet Chestnut, Holly. The 3 G-forces of Love (Gratitude, Grace and Generosity): Tulips, Carnation, Chicory.

Food

Lots of green vegetables such as avocado, broccoli, green capsicum, zucchini, cucumber, spinach, baby spinach, string beans, spring onions, leeks, bok choy, cabbage, snow peas, sugar snag peas, sprouts and lettuce. Fills jars with water and allow bunches of herbs to cascade over the sides: mint, parsley, chives, dandelion greens, basil, sage, thyme, coriander… you get the picture. Fruits to snack on during the day include Granny Smith apples, pears, honeydew melon, grapes, limes and kiwi fruit. Drink green tea if you're after a hot drink, or water infused with mint leaves if you're after something more refreshing.

Element

Air. When feeling as light as a feather, your heart is open to all the joy the Universe has to offer. Air represents lightness, freedom, subtlety and infinite exchange, whereas wind can range from a natural energy source to a destructive cyclone. The winds of change can extinguish or fuel our fire, but too much can lead to burn out. Likewise, too much air and we become air-headed – beings without substance. Every minute of every day we inhale, we exhale, inhale, exhale… we can do it passively and let it keep us alive, or we can do it consciously and feel alive. Be conscious of your breath – keep it measured and deep. Items you can put on your altar include feathers, balloons, a fan, leaves that you have seen falling from a tree.

Direction

East. East is associated with the rising sun, the element of Air and the new dawn in the wheel of the year. Spring represents renewed hope, wonder, illumination, and a sense of anticipation. It is a beginning of knowing and loving who we are to prepare us for the rest of our journey. Add an arrangement of fresh flowers to your altar as a centrepiece, lay a spring of cherry blossoms in your East corner, or scatter petals across your directions. Other include fluffy feathers, a packet of seeds, or a dusted-off bikini!

Animals

For an animal to encompass all that the heart chakra represents, it must be giving and revitalising, unconditional and empathetic in nature. Scott associates the heart chakra with Dog, Lady Beetle, Frog and Dove.

Symbols

The symbol of the heart chakra is often that of a 12-pointed lotus encasing a six-pointed star. The numbers themselves suggest balance and duality, divisible yet intertwined. Six is the number of co-operation, accord, peace, goodness, beauty and truth. The number 12 is symbolic of God's perfect government – 12 tribes, 12 gates to the city of God, 12 apostles, 12 zodiac signs in his heavens.

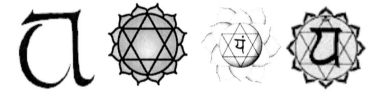

Mother Earth

Glastonbury, England Glastonbury is the legendary burial place of King Arthur, and is located in the south west of England. Of particular significance is the Glastonbury Tor, at the summit of which sits the remnants of St Michael's church. The Tor is just one of the many sacred sites lying in the path of the Michael and Mary ley lines, and is a magnet to people of faith.

There is an annual event in Glastonbury known as the Glastonbury Pilgrimage, which has been attracting Christians since 1924. Each year worshippers travel to the county of Somerset to express their personal faith.

Throat Chakra :: Thursday

The throat chakra is related to communication, courage, inspiration and creative connection. It assists with clairaudience, which is the ability to hear on the non-physical planes. Trust and honour higher forces at work within you to keep your throat chakra open and vibrant.

Thursday is a fabulous day for working with throat chakra energy as it is named after Jupiter – the planet that signifies expansion and growth. Jupiter represents strong morals, prosperity, maturity, dependability and luck. And the throat chakra, coincidentally, is related to communication, courage, inspiration and creative connection.

Positive Traits

This chakra facilitates diplomatic and graceful expression. It gives you the courage and diplomacy to say what needs to be said without the fear of consequence. When you know how to ask for your own way, chances are you'll get it. Your excellent wit and style helps you articulate your mission, build bridges between parties, and become a leader amongst your team players.

Hard-working, loyal and trustworthy, people have a strong sense of right and wrong and therefore make great devil's advocates. They are committed to seeing projects through, whether they be business oriented or personal relationships. Not surprisingly, these people make fabulous orators, emcees, motivational speakers, teachers, preachers and singers.

When Out of Balance...

Nagging or hen-pecking is a sign of a throat chakra in need of attention. Same deal if you find yourself enforcing your opinion onto others or talking in a defensive, suspicious or anxious manner. Other symptoms of an imbalanced throat chakra include greed, arrogance and an inability to ask for help.

Further indicators include repressing anger through denial, evasive sweet talk, going into the 'silent treatment' mode, biting your tongue to keep the peace, taking the higher ground and preaching at others, or blaming yourself for others' problems. This turns into throat problems, speech impediments or tight muscles in the jaw or shoulders. If you question everything, ask yourself, "how does it serve me to doubt?"

The Throat Chakra as Part of Your Life Journey

The old 'children are to be seen and not heard' idiom taught us that our voice was redundant and to suppress our true feelings. It also causes some children to become habitual liars as they are taught to suppress their truth. This is not a good start for those of us reaching full adulthood, the life stage housed in the throat chakra. From this age we are learning to talk about our own experiences, aligning our speech with that which others want to hear, rather than the ego-centric "me-me-me" talk of a teenager. Gregariousness grows, as does the skill of effective communication. We also stop the white lies, cease coughing or choking when it comes to sharing our feelings or needs, and laughter is only for joy (not for masking shyness).

Tools for the Throat Chakra

Colour

Sky Blue. Light blue – the colour of the sky – is associated with coolness, inner peace and mental clarity. It is also good for introspection due to its reflective qualities. As opposed to emotionally warm colours like red, orange, and yellow, light blue influences intellect and logic. Use light blue to promote the flow of communication at home or at work, to ease depression (the 'blues'), to promote loyalty, and to broaden your perspective of your world.

Essential Oils

Vetiver as a deeply nourishing promoter of opportunities and possibilities, is used with cedarwood to decongest the chakra. This allows lemon and cajeput to bring clarity and vision, lavender to balance your new energy, and frankincense to rejuvenate intentions.

Gemstones

Blue gemstones help calm troubled waters through the use of words and actions. Wear throat chakra gemstones around your neck to help your words and ideas flow smoothly, or as earrings – this will help you hear as well as speak. Try Blue Lace Agate, Celestite, Lapis Lazuli, Aquamarine or Turquoise.

Sound

This is the perfect opportunity to really get those vocal chords vibrating! You can take it easy and hum along to crystal bowls in the tone of G, hum the mantra 'ham' or the vowel 'u' as in blue. Alternatively, chant the sacred vowel of RE. Ramp things up a bit and sing your favourite songs at the top of your voice. Enjoy sing-alongs with your children and teach them the value of letting it all out. Howl at the moon, sing the sun awake. Pretend you're Liza Minelli and kick your legs high to cabaret, show tunes, freedom songs, and gospel music.

Archetypal Goddess

There are many goddesses who rule over the domain of self-expression, such as Athena, Fortuna, Rhiannon, Dana, Demeter, Iambe and Oshun.. They teach us how to ask for things for our highest good, and how our expressions manifest in exactly the way we describe. They teach us to settle differences, bridge the divide between the genders, the generations and the ignorant, and how to foster healing at all levels.

Intention

Use key words around self-expression, truth, diplomacy and being heard. Themes for release include unfair compromise, conditioned silence, denial, old habits and lies.

Sense

Hearing. Just as a healthy throat chakra enables you to listen to your authentic self and express your needs beautifully, it also helps you listen to and more importantly, hear, others.

Flowers

The light-blue forget-me-not is a symbolic flower for *remembering* – wearing a forget-me-not on your lapel says that you are consciously keeping a loved one in your heart, and that his or her story lives on through you. Blue plants can create a cool, soothing effect, and if planted with white flowers, can create an appearance of water. The energy associated with water, of course, is energy flow – a vital aspect when considering the expression of ideas and thoughts. Mimulus, Agrimony, Beech, Kangaroo Paw.

Food

The higher three chakras are associated with the physical functions of breathing, hearing, thinking and sleep-wake cycles.

Choose foods that promote the health of these functions: Foods high in vitamin C (orange juice, broccoli, tomato, papaya, mango and kiwi fruit); high in vitamin E (wheat germ oil, almonds, peanuts and spinach); high in omega-3 fatty acids (salmon, sardines, trout, walnuts, soy beans, tofu and flaxseed oil); high in anti-oxidants (green tea, red onions, blueberries, cranberries, red grapes, kidney beans, garlic, ginger and red wine.

On a metaphysical level, choose foods that are crunchy, tart or tangy, quenching and fresh.

Element

Sound travels in waves and carries messages that connect our minds and bodies to our surroundings. We are able to discern danger, feel peace or detect opportunities for joy. Sound also facilitates communication between us. We can express our needs, desires and creative ideas, and at the same time, hear these things from others.

Direction

North. North is associated with the height of summer, the heat of the midday sun, and the sense of being full. Summer, in turn, represents maturity, passion, courage, enthusiasm and all the energy and ability you need to do everything you want to do. Self-confidence abounds and manifests as benevolence, infectious optimism and inspired creativity. Add items to symbolise the sun and summer to your altar – sunglasses, a sun visor, beach sand or, if you can find one, a mini sun dial. Contrast this with blue and turquoise items to represent the sky and the sea.

Animals

The animals Scott Alexander King thinks of when pondering the throat chakra are persuasive and strong, honourable and brave. They espouse the need to be heard, while inspiring a deep sense of honour and respect for our self and others. Scott suggests Lion and Eagle are appropriate for this purpose.

Symbols

Throat chakra symbol has sixteen petals, one for each of the 16 Sanskrit vowels. Often the throat chakra is also depicted with a downward-pointing triangle (spirit), and a circle within the triangle (eternity or the full moon). I have seen personal interpretations using musical notes, a mouth, and even an apple (to represent an Adam's apple).

Mother Earth

The Great Pyramid of Giza, Mount Sinai, and the Mount of Olives are significant landmarks in Egypt and Israel are inexorably linked in the biblical story of the Exodus – the forty year journey of Moses and the Jews from Egypt to the Promised Land. Mount Sinai is the home to the cave where Moses waited to receive the Ten Commandments, and Jesus is said to have spent a good deal of time prophesising on the Mount of Olives. The messages given and received were of love, healing and peace, yet the modern Middle East is suffering from war, decay and death.

Third-Eye Chakra :: Friday

The third eye chakra is related to the act of seeing, both physically and intuitively. As such it broadens your viewpoints, expands your ability to see beyond obvious perspectives, and unleashes your understanding of where you fit in the world. The awakening of this chakra also leads to clairvoyance, stimulates your psychic faculties and fuels your ability to see on the non-physical planes.

Friday was named after Freja, the Scandinavian goddess of passion, love and war. It is a day also named after the planet Venus, whose properties includes love, beauty, values and comfort. With patronesses like these, this is a day to explore the highest possibilities to the highest degree for your highest good. Think bigger, better, onwards and upwards.

Positive Traits

When vibrant and alert a balanced third eye chakra allows us to experience clarity. In effect, we become able to understand our life purpose. It also assists in studies, negotiations and communication of truth, whether that be through words, pictures or by channelling divine messages.

Highly attuned third-eye people tend to be sensitive, romantic, insightful and honest. They strive for a life beyond the mundane and are therefore are unique in their way of thinking or expressing their ideas. Often, they are a source of comfort to those around them for their calmness, gifted insight, wisdom and diplomacy. As such, they make fabulous artists and musicians, psychics, social workers, creative writers and primary school teachers.

When Out of Balance…

Any self-doubt is a guaranteed way to block the third-eye chakra – by shutting down your instincts and inherent wisdom, you effectively block your third eye chakra. This manifests as vanity, laziness, lethargy, moodiness and a tendency to live in the past. You might also suffer from a poor or hazy memory, be 'one-eyed' (stubborn) about some issues, and run chronically late for appointments. Don't get so self-absorbed that you alienate yourself from others, get lost in the maze you have created for yourself, or lose sleep from holding negative thoughts in your mind. Mind too, that you don't jump to conclusions.

The Third Eye Chakra as Part of Your Life Journey

As we grow older our thoughts turn to self-reflection as we examines our life's purpose. Such awareness raises the vibration of the third eye chakra so that you are able to detach from trivia and see the bigger picture. You can consciously release the limitations of cultural conditioning, family influence and even time as you pursue only knowledge that is true. We begin to identify and reverse destructive habits, but this generally begins to happen naturally after the age of thirty. At this stage, you are learning why you are conforming rather than honouring your truth, and having the creative capacity to think of alternative options.

As you enter the wise woman / wise man stage of your life, acknowledge that the choices you have made are perfect although some of them may not seem so at the time. At this life stage it is easy to remember and appreciate that you wouldn't be the beautiful being you are today without some of the hardships or experiences your choices exposed you to.

A healthy third-eye chakra allows you to accept that everything happens at the perfect time for the perfect reason, and so you can stop fretting about decisions.

Tools for the Third-Eye Chakra

Colour

Indigo. Indigo (a darker blue) represents the infinite boundaries of the evening sky – oftentimes staring at the heavens is a time for reflection and for gleaning insights. Indigo, therefore, symbolises confidence, wisdom, faith, loyalty, trust and integrity. As this chakra is the seat of our insightful-ness, indigo represents those ideas that come 'out of the blue'. Therefore, add indigo to your life when you want to develop your intuition, rise above the rut you have created for yourself, enjoy solitude, or find a solution to a problem.

Essential Oils

Cedarwood unblocks energy log-jams ready for rosemary (a brain stimulant that promotes clarity), calming lavender, frankincense and lemon (for rejuvenation), and basil to assist with decision making in your new space of vision and insight. Psychics, mediums, meditation groups and students also love using this blend for the sense of lucidity they are able to achieve. Students can read and remember their work while cramming for exams, and people working on their intuition skills are able to enter a beautiful space without the noise and encumbrances of daily life.

Gemstones

Not surprisingly, it is the dark blue gemstones that facilitate the opening of the subconscious, and the sense of peace and understanding. Moonstone, Sodalite, Dark Aquamarine, Azurite, Sapphire, Kyanite.

Sound

Play meditative music that allows your mind to roam, explore possibilities and find answers out of the blue. Teach your children to sing the alphabet, and see if you can challenge your intellect to sing it backwards. For a gentler experience, you can play crystal bowls in the tone of A, and chant the sacred vowel of AH. Or, for an energetic, insightful, positive and affirming experience, you can add the suggested songs to your playlist. I've included songs about crying to help you clear energy on a physical level – crying is very cleansing and uplifting, and a beautiful way to shift blockages.

Archetypal Goddess

"To thine own self be true," says Shakespeare, as do the many goddesses who rule over the domain of self-reflection: Isis, Hathor, Baba Yaga, Cerridwen, Brigid, Inanna and Epona.
A person whose third eye is open is able to make decisions with clarity and absolute trust in her own innate wisdom.

Intention

Here is your chance to create an affirmation that will banish procrastination and self-doubt for good. Focus on bringing mental and intuitive clarity into your life and on the benefits you will receive in doing this.

Sense

Sixth. The third eye chakra rules a very powerful skill that lies dormant in many people – an inherent ability to trust, and to see beyond what our physical eyes show us. Call it extra-sensory perception (ESP), telepathy, clairvoyance, other-worldliness, second sight, channelling or simply a hunch, your sixth sense lies latent within 85 percent of your brain. Some liken the process of 'tuning in' to that of tuning in your radio. Know where you want to finish up on the dial for the transmission to come though.

Flowers

Often when something happens to us, we mull the incident over and over until it becomes distorted or represented as a new truth. In our mind, we tease, stretch, chew and skew the experience until we end up with a convoluted version of the original truth. Use the following flowers to promote clarity and trust and to release habits of toxic thinking. Agrimony, Wild Oat, Nasturtium, Geranium, Chestnut Bud, Scleranthus, White Chestnut.

Food

The third eye chakra in particular is related to the ears and brain. The relationship between what we eat and how we think, act, and learn is inexorably linked. New Scientist magazine published a story in May 2005 called "11 Steps to a Better Brain" which examines the effect of food on the grey matter. Food with slow-release sugars and fish are the best source of brain food, while junk food (and highly processed food) is detrimental to mental health. So to boost memory, increase your attention span, improve your concentration and become more alert: Eat grapes, blueberries, eggplant and purple cabbage contain a dark blue to purple pigment called anthocyanin which are considered mental health boosters; Eliminate white foods (high in simple carbohydrates, or quick-release sugars) from your day – choose wholemeal (brown foods); Eat fish, or at least take a fish oil supplement; Eat vegetables that improve brain function – broccoli, tomatoes, chillies and sweet potato – the brighter the colour (dark green, deep purple), the better; Drink grape juice.

Element

Light. When God said, "Let there be light," light came before anything else in the creation of humanity. As such, illumination, both physically and philosophically, is paramount to human psyche. To be in the dark is to feel isolated and confused. Banish dark thoughts, recognise and release self-sabotaging intentions, and become conscious of automatic habits. See green traffic lights everywhere you go. Naturally, a lamp, torch, light globes, fairy-lights or candles are ideal items to place on your altar.

Direction

Within. After the high energy of summer, there comes a time to balance your energies by digging in – entering a state of meditative withdrawal and self-reflection. It is completely healthy to enjoy Me Time away from the constant pressures of work or home. Life goes on with or without you, so know that when you go Within, it is your gift to the world when you emerge refreshed and centred. Altar items may represent acts of self-indulgence – manicure tools, favourite books or magazines, exotic moisturising crème, your photo albums, or even your well-worn hiking boots.

Animals

Work with animals that are super sensitive to their environment, those around them and the subtler realms of existence. Scott suggests working with Dolphin, Swan and Dragonfly.

Symbols

The third eye chakra is often portrayed with two white lotus petals that look like wings. A golden downward-pointing triangle stands for divine perfection, but could also signify your holy trinity – faith/ hope/ love; past/ present/ future; or the maiden/ mother/ crone triple goddess, to name a few allegories. Sometimes you'll see the third eye depicted as an actual eye. Some artists include a crescent moon and the dot of manifestation, or incredibly, 96 petals. Many artists avoid putting the third eye symbol in a circle (unlike the first five chakras) because they don't want the expanse of their consciousness confined by a border.

Mother Earth

Wherever Your Intuition Says It Is! For healing your third eye chakra, the seat of your intuition and natural wisdom, please locate a place where you feel free of earthly concerns. Don't spend too long thinking about where this place should be. Whatever comes to mind immediately is usually correct. If you get really stuck, however, take a look at the website of Dan Shaw, a modern alchemist and publisher of Vortex Maps. Dan has done oodles of research into the earth's vortices and has identified 'vile' and 'cool' vortexes around the world – the large stone monuments located at equidistant points around the globe, Sedona (Arizona), in the Himalayas, within the Incan culture in Peru, are examples of cool vortexes.

Crown Chakra :: Saturday

There are many forms of knowledge – cognitive, emotional, intuitive, learned, to name a few. But wisdom is a new level of understanding that transcends the physical plane. And so, when awakened, this chakra brings us such wisdom, knowledge, understanding, spiritual connection, and bliss.

Work with this chakra on Saturday – the day named after Saturn, whose properties are discipline, patience and perseverance. In ancient times it was the furthest planet that could be seen by the naked eye. Its seemingly infinite journey around the Sun connects us to a greater world beyond, to a timeless, spaceless place of all-knowing. As does the crown chakra, which becomes our channel to pure awareness through consciousness.

Positive Traits

A healthy crown chakra is associated with the ability to consciously travel on the non-physical planes (astral travel). But it also enables us to experience a connection to your faith, whether that be a god, goddess, spirit, angels, Universe or your higher self. Such a connection brings peace to your life, understandably. It helps you be that friendly, easy-going and genuine person you've always wanted to be.

Crown chakra people are accepting, trusting, emotionally involved in all their relationships, and understand many points of view. As such, they make great master teachers, humanitarians and mediators. They are also natural artists, musicians, healers and peacekeepers.

When Out of Balance...

If you've been described as an airhead, chances are you haven't even absorbed this name-calling as you avoid conflict at all cost. This isn't such a bad thing, unless you are one for always getting lost in the clouds with your idealism.

On the other end of the scale, you know when your crown chakra is out of balance when you attempt to stop new thoughts, whether they're your own or belong to others. You become sceptic, apathetic, and overly concerned with material wealth. This is because highly sensitive people can feel trapped by authority. The perceived negative higher power threatens their fantasy world and can lead to a state of catastrophe, stubbornness, isolation and separation.

Perhaps you have a creative block or lost your spiritual connection. Instead of building your castle in the air, consider laying foundations on the earth first.

The Crown Chakra as Part of Your Life Journey

Many children have imaginary friends, play with fairies at the bottom of the garden, or see puppets as real entities. If these beliefs are ridiculed during childhood, it can be difficult to feel comfortable with the limitless freedom of the imagination later in life. On a more earthly level, it can lead to a bunch of negative thoughts cluttering your mind. This manifests as sleeplessness, anxiety, or eating disorders due to a lack of self awareness. You may also experience poor balance, co-ordination difficulties and clumsiness.

Ultimately, your life becomes limited, routine and unremarkable. You might even have a self-limiting belief that no-one in this world supports you, or that God has forsaken you. If so, are you ready to make your life remarkable? Why haven't you taken this step, so far?

Before you blame a higher power for negative experiences and loss of innocence, ask yourself, where did you learn how to blame in the first place? The answer lies in your the social conditioning you were exposed to during your journey. Allow time to address issues that prevent you from being happy so that you may enter the seventh stage of life with peace of mind.

Tools for the Crown Chakra

Colour

Purple is the colour of royalty, and violet represents spiritual mastery – both colours are used to correspond with the crown chakra. Add shades of purple to your life when you want to expand your imagination, remove obstacles, and feel like royalty. Purple is blended from red (energy) and blue (spirit) so represents your Self and your soul, dignity, mystery and magic. It is an excellent colour to relieve headaches, promote faith and to fuse your physical self with higher spiritual consciousness. Darker tones are associated with gloom and sorrow, whereas the lighter tone of pale lilac stands for love of humanity, femininity, nostalgia and cosmic affiliation. Sometimes the crown chakra is represented with all the colours of the rainbow shooting out from the crown into the heavens. So this time you have a choice about colours you use for your journal – you can stick with purple tones, or go the whole gamut and have a blast with every colour in your palette.

Essential Oils

A euphoric state of enlightenment can be achieved through the combination of peppermint, clove leaf and cinnamon bark. Blend this combination with sweet orange to keep you relaxed in this heightened state. People who love this blend describe a gorgeous feeling of connection with God/dess, Angels, Spirit, Universe, or whatever their faith system is.

Gemstones

Purple gemstones are used for meditation for their properties of mysticism and purification. A stone under your pillow as you sleep, or keeping it on your deck of tarot cards, will help you connect with your purpose. Amethyst, Sugilite, Iolite, Chalcedony, Fluorite.

Sound

Experiment with choir, gospel and chill-out grooves – whatever music form inspires you to look to the heavens, wave your arms in the air, and abandon your entire self to the feeling of ecstasy. For a group meditation, you can play crystal bowls in the tone of B, and chant the sacred vowel of OM. This mantra is used by many traditions to achieve theta wave consciousness, and is especially powerful when performed by a group.

Archetypal Goddess

Crown chakra goddesses preside over the domain of self-knowledge. They help you see yourself as a minute organism in the ways of the world, both in the physical and non-physical planes, in the present and the future. Disconnecting with the world every now and then can be healthy if it lets you travel to a spaceless, timeless place of knowledge, wisdom, understanding and spiritual connection. The crown chakra energy can also be associated with the more magical, cosmic and crone goddesses. Nuit, Spider Woman, Circe, Hecate, IxChel, Yemaya, Bast.

Intention

What is your highest potential? Trust that what you ask for is exactly what the Universe is waiting to bring you! Spread your wings and create an affirmation that is as uplifting and bliss-packed as you can imagine.

Sense

Extra-Sensory. Have you ever woken up and felt sure, really sure, that your dreams were so lucid that it's the act of waking up that feels unreal? If so, it is possible you spent the night astral travelling – an out-of-body experience whereby your soul transcends into an astral body and projects itself into a parallel world or the astral plane. Also known as astral projection or soul travel, the journey may be felt by the physical body and remembered by the conscious mind.

Flowers

Purple flowers generally represent dignity, pride and success due to the colour's implication of royalty. Purple in name and nature, for example, Violets give you a sense of understanding of the world, your life and you. Lilacs, Irises, Hydrangeas, African Violets are other purple flowers. Other flower essences valuable to the crown chakra include White Chestnut, Sweet Chestnut, Cerato, Mustard, Dahlia, Honeysuckle.

Food

Bliss out on your favourite foods today, consciously bless your food before eating, and shower blessings upon every person who contributed their energy in bringing the food to you – from the farmer to the truck driver to the cook to the friends you are sharing with, be generous with your wishes. Purple foods such as eggplants, grapes, plums, cabbage, and beets aside, focus on the one, fabulous recipe you can do really well. When you prepare it today, infuse your actions with heaven-sent intentions. If you're feeling adventurous, perhaps even explore cooking Tibetan food in honour of the earth's crown chakra, Mount Kailas in Tibet. Whatever you do, keep it Simple, Simple, Simple.

Burn or hang incense and smudging herbs as you cook. Try sage, copal, myrrh, frankincense and juniper. Don't eat them, simply, have them around you as you cook for purification.

Element

Faith / Spirit. The crucial element that separates humans from every other creature on the planet is that humans have the ability to think independently, logically and constructively. We are gifted with the ability to think cognitively, creatively and spiritually. Know that you deserve the best of everything so that Universe can deliver this to you. Place a journal, letters, pen and paper, spider's web or a dream catcher on your altar as items symbolising the gift of positive thinking.

Direction

Above. Hopefully, at least once in your life, you will have experienced the all-freeing, enlightening feeling of blissing out; of absolutely knowing that all is right with your world; that right here, right now, everything is perfect. The purpose of giving time and intention to the Above direction is to invite these feelings back into your life. Look upwards to look forward, think optimistically, and feel positively confident about your destiny. What item or image can you add to altar that makes you giddy with happiness, alive with purpose and secure in your faith?

Animals

The crown chakra helps us to comprehend and surrender to the 'Great Mystery', the Void and all that is known to be unknowable. Black animals are typically considered messengers of the Void, and therefore, totems of the crown chakra because of their mysterious, Otherworldly appearance and their ability to hide in the shadows. Crow, Magpie, Unicorn and Dragon are perfect.

Symbols

The Sanskrit name for the crown chakra is Sahasrara, meaning 'thousandfold'. This is why you'll often see this chakra represented as a thousand-petaled lotus. Having never personally counted 1000 petals, however, I prefer to see the petals as an infinite number symbolising the infinite nature of this chakra and its spiritual aspects. Some think of the crown chakra symbol as the halo around Jesus' head. A friend of mine sees a well when she thinks of this chakra, which represents the bottomless depths from which intuitive knowledge can be drawn.

Mother Earth

Mount Kailas, Tibet At the time of writing this book, Tor Webster has not yet visited the sacred site of Mount Kailas in far western Tibet. But that's not really surprising – only a few thousand pilgrims visit this very sacred and remote mountain each year. This is no reflection on the deep sacredness with which the landmark is held by Hindus, Buddhists, Jains and Tibetans. It is an arduous journey to Mt Kailas, but for those who manage it, the reward is said to be spectacular scenery and a life-changing experience.

The Tibetan word for pilgrimage, neykhor, means to 'circle around a sacred place' – a similar concept to our expression, 'happiness is the journey, not the destination'. Once around is not enough for the Tibetans – they believe that enlightenment is assured to those who complete 108 journeys around the mountain.

Taking the journey from ignorance to enlightenment is to transcend through the attachments of the materialistic world to a state of higher consciousness and illumination.

Notes

Notes

Notes

About the Author

Anita Revel is the author of a growing collection of well-being resources in various forms of manifestation, countless columns for United Press International, hundreds of articles found sprinkled across the internet, and numerous books for women's well-being.

Anita lives on a farm in the stunning Margaret River region of Western Australia with her husband, two children and a dog who is as loyal as his nearest cuddle. You can visit her at AnitaRevel.com

For further study opportunities, try the **Goddess Makeover Home-Study Course in Personal Values, Self-Realisation and Divine Revellion** by Anita Revel. Create a personal values totem and realise your inner wow-factor in just seven lessons. To enrol, visit

GoddessMakeover.com

CPSIA information can be obtained at www.ICGtesting.com
Printed in the USA
LVOW132328140413

329122LV00002B/243/P